From the Author

Andrea D. Merriman

With / Dr. Raymond Youngblood, Jr.

Anticipating The Pain

Instead Of Accepting The Love

Publishing by YOUNGBLOOD

WORLDWIDE - INTERNATIONAL

Title: Anticipating The Pain Instead Of Accepting The Love
Authors: Andrea D. Merriman | Dr. Raymond Youngblood, Jr.
Certain content definitions provided by general public sources.

ISBN: 978-1-952039-23-2
(Paperback)

Designed by Publishing by YOUNGBLOOD
Editing and Content Enhanced by Youngblood Industries AI
Cover Design by Office For Arts
Photos Credit by unless otherwise credited, all photos are from the author s collection.
Digital Artwork by Office For Arts

Email to: PublishingByYoungblood@Gmail.Com

Subjects: LCSH: Self-actualization (Psychology) | Self-control | Motivation (Psychology) | Success
BISAC: Self-Help / Personal Growth / Success / Motivational & Inspirational

H.E.L.P.®

Offering Hope, Empowerment, Life Skills & Prevention

FEMININE LIFE REBUILDERS™

FLR Global Institute, LLC

www.jymhelpprogram.com

This Book Is Brought to You in Collaboration with
Youngblood Industries—YGB Hybrid Currency

You can't treat us like everyone else because we're not like anyone else.

The YGB Hybrid Currency is a hybrid currency system that attaches minerals, metals, natural resources, and other physical assets to technological applications, creating a more stable and secure currency by grounding its value in tangible assets. It was created by gold miner Dr. Raymond Youngblood, Jr.

www.YoungbloodIndustries.com

Publishing by **YOUNGBLOOD**

Make A Promise To Yourself

Before you go any further, take a moment—right here and right now—to make a promise to yourself. Promise that when you reach the final page of this book, you won't just close it and move on. You will hold onto the commitment you made today and carry it forward. The words ahead aren't just meant to be read; they're meant to inspire action. So, make that promise, and when you're done, keep it.

I promise (write your words here.):

_____

_____

_____

_____

_____

_____.

Nothing will stop me from fulfilling this promise!

Content

Dedication

When I was searching for a house, one of the features I desired was a picture window. I enjoy looking out the window and watching my children play. Now, I can see my grandchildren having fun on the trampoline while I stand at the kitchen sink.

The amusing part is that they can also see me and wave. When they are in the yard, they look up and wave enthusiastically to ensure I notice them. So, that window truly looks both ways.

Writing this book has felt like standing in the picture window of my life, watching my past unfold like a movie. Like watching my grandkids, I am opening myself up for you to glimpse my world.

As you look into my world, allow me to express my appreciation to the men and women who have contributed to this process. I sincerely thank all of you. Four women have consistently supported me through all my challenges, and I dedicate this book to them.

First, my mother, Nanette Whitney, has always been my saving grace. Even at 97, as she battles Alzheimer's, her quick wit still reveals a woman of class. Her wisdom throughout my life and how she shares it has always inspired me to become a better woman. Her dedication to family and community has set a high standard for me and many others. Friends often say, "I want to be like Ms. Nanette when I grow up." She truly is a pearl of great price.

Next are my sisters, Deadra Hall and Marcia Helms. They embody sisterhood. I couldn't have asked for a better support system if I had handpicked them according to my requirements. They helped raise and protect me; to this day, they are just a phone call away.

Then there is Vanessa Fuqua. For 50 years, we have cried, laughed, and prayed through every relationship—good, bad, and indifferent. We have shared moments of silence and have taken turns playing the "good person" role, allowing the other to vent.

Thank you, ladies. I am here today because of your love, support, and prayers. Because of you, I can be a leader2, mother, grandmother, sister, and friend. Your love shines through me, and with you in my life, I know I have favor from God.

From My Journal

I have never felt more vulnerable as I extract materials from my journal. You must know how far I have come to trust you. Choosing the right words is another challenge. How do I communicate with you? I want to guide you on your path, yet I'm hesitant to expose all my vulnerabilities. The only way I know to help you is to expose myself, my past, and my emotions. I know nothing great comes without a cost. I expect to receive harsh criticism from some people and love from others. But I also know that my openness can uplift others. It's more than joy for me. It's moving forward for you. In the worst of it, somewhere, someone will think, "If she can do it, so can I." I hope that's you.

This isn't just about my vulnerabilities, which I write about in my journal; it's our story. It reflects the experiences of many others who have endured pain and trauma and poured themselves into caring for others only to struggle to believe they deserve love—or worse, not know they deserve love. You deserve love.

It speaks to the women who give until empty, with nothing left, completely drained until they no longer have an identity. To the men who fear vulnerability, a fear that you are somehow less of a man if you show emotions. To anyone who has ever sabotaged their chance at happiness out of fear of the unknown, not wanting to disappoint others, or being stuck in a state of being a giver without ever knowing how to receive. I reached back many years into my journal for you.

Writing this book felt like standing before a picture window, watching my past being played out in front of me. You see how small, innocent, and vulnerable you are. You also get to see all the people around you: those who didn't know what they were doing, those who ignored you, and those who made every attempt to protect you from others or yourself.

Just as I enjoy watching my grandkids on the trampoline, knowing they can see me, too, I realize that sharing these pages means opening up my world to you and yours to me. Reflection is a two-way window. I recognize what was and how those moments shaped me through revisiting my memories. As you read, you stand on the other side, looking in. I see you; our story will be in the same journal. Understand that this is the beginning.

Introduction: Anticipating the Pain Instead of Accepting the Love

Anticipating the pain—a torment in itself. It's slow, a relentless approach that does not crash but enters with a noisy creep instead. You see it coming; it doesn't hide, seeping into the bones, poisoning your mentality, and twisting your personality too tight to untangle. When the full effect finally arrives—the pain breaks you and numbs you; it always hurts you the same, no matter how many times it occurs. Instead of accepting love, an offering of solace and warmth, you retreat into the isolation of hurt and its familiarity with the pain.

For much of my life, I've been the one who gives in relationships—the one who freely offers love, energy, patience, and understanding, yet rarely receives anything in return. This pattern has occurred so often that I feel guilt or shame whenever someone gives something back. If you're reading this, you might relate to this struggle, feeling like you're the only one giving in your relationships. You're not alone. Your struggle is valid, and it's okay to feel this way. I understand the struggle of giving too much and not receiving enough in return. It's a valid struggle, and you're not alone in it. Your feelings are valid, and you are not alone in this struggle.

The Givers Dilemma

For years, I've been the one who gives in relationships, loves, sacrifices, and bends to make things work. I've been the rock, the nurturer, and the problem solver. And in return? Silence, neglect, or, at best, a vague acknowledgment of my efforts. I told myself that love was about giving, not receiving. I even believed I could find peace if the other person were happy.

The 'Givers Dilemma 'is a crucial concept that can help us better understand our relationships. It's a situation where one person in a relationship gives more than they receive, often leading to feelings of imbalance and unfulfillment.

But deep down, I always knew something was missing.

One day, it hit me. Me! What about me? When do I get to feel loved? It wasn't just a fleeting question. It was a gut-wrenching realization that I had ignored my own needs for far too long. But it's never too late to start accepting and prioritizing your needs. This is a journey of self-awareness, self-acceptance, and it's a journey worth taking.

Traumas Grip

They say trauma traps you in the past, and I now see how true that is. When I'm with a man who can love me in ways I've never known, I feel like a silly, lovestruck teenager. I blush, fumble, and second-guess myself. I can't reconcile this behavior with the fact that I'm older and more experienced. Instead of stepping into love confidently, I shrink back, anticipating the pain I've grown accustomed to. This is what I call 'Trauma's Grip, 'the lingering influence of past experiences that can shape our present feelings and behaviors, often leading us to anticipate adverse outcomes even when positive ones are possible.

It was as if I was stuck in the mindset of my younger self, the one who first learned to fear rejection, loss, and heartbreak. No matter how much I grow, trauma whispers that love is dangerous and that happiness is fleeting.

Healthy Boundaries

Healthy boundaries are the foundation of strong, respectful relationships. They define how we protect our emotional well-being while fostering trust, connection, and mutual understanding. Whether building new relationships or repairing old ones, clear boundaries help prevent resentment, miscommunication, and burnout. Boundaries are not about shutting people out; they create space for authenticity, respect, and growth. We will explore establishing healthy boundaries supporting meaningful and lasting connections.

The Burden of Being the Helper

Over the years, I've become the go-to person for relationship advice. Women call me about their husbands, seeking wisdom and clarity. Sometimes, the men encourage it, telling their wives to call Andrea. Maybe she'll get through to you. I've been the mediator, the encourager, and the friend who helps others untangle their relationship struggles. This role, while fulfilling in some ways, can also become a burden. It can lead to neglecting one's own needs and using the act of helping others as a distraction from personal issues. This is what I call the 'Burden of Being the Helper,' a situation where helping others becomes a way to avoid addressing one's own needs and issues, leading to a sense of unfulfillment and imbalance in one's life. But it's essential to recognize if you're in this situation and take steps to address your own needs. You can control your needs and issues, and it's empowering to do so.

But here's the irony: while I can guide others to healthier relationships, I've struggled to find that same health and balance for myself. I've used helping others to distract myself from my own needs. Giving to others temporarily filled the void but never healed the deeper wounds. It's a stark realization that I've been neglecting my needs, and it's a powerful wake-up call to start prioritizing self-care. You have the power to prioritize your own needs and take care of yourself. If you find navigating this journey challenging, don't hesitate to seek professional help. A therapist or counselor can provide you with the necessary support and guidance to heal and build healthier relationships.

The Crossroads

Now, I'm faced with something unfamiliar: the possibility of being on the receiving end of love, of being seen, valued, and cherished for who I am. Instead of celebrating this, I find myself bracing for the inevitable heartbreak. But what if, just for a moment, I allowed myself to believe that this love could be real? That I could be worthy of it? I spent so long anticipating the pain that I didn't know how to accept the love. But now, I see a glimmer of hope, a possibility of a different future. This is not just a possibility; it's a promise of a different, more fulfilling future. This realization can inspire us to believe in the possibility of a healthier, more balanced relationship.

There is hope for a different, more fulfilling future, and it's within your reach. This is the crossroads I find myself at now. Do I keep repeating the same patterns, loving others to distract myself from my needs, anticipating hurt even when love is offered, or do I risk genuinely letting someone in? This is a crucial point in the healing journey, where one must decide whether to continue the familiar but unfulfilling patterns or take a leap of faith toward a healthier, more balanced relationship. I pose a question to you, the reader: do you dare to believe that you are worthy of receiving the same love you have so freely given to others? It's a question that invites reflection and self-discovery. Take a moment to reflect on the patterns in your relationships. You can shape your healing journey through self-reflection and self-discovery.

What About Me

Anticipating the Pain Instead of Accepting the Love is not just my story; it is the story of so many others who have lived through trauma, poured themselves into others, and struggled to believe they deserve love. But here's the thing: it is possible to reclaim love. It is for the women who give until they are empty, the men who fear vulnerability, and anyone who has ever sabotaged their chance at happiness because they were too afraid of the unknown. This book is a beacon of hope, showing that breaking free from these patterns is possible and finding the love and healing you deserve.

There is a path to healing; it's within your reach.

For far too long, you have been conditioned to believe that putting others first was noble, that enduring your pain quietly was a badge of honor, and that sacrificing yourself in the name of love somehow made you worthy. But let me tell you something: this isn't strength. Its self-destruction. You have been playing the role of the martyr, convinced that your suffering makes you unique, but in reality, it only keeps you trapped in a cycle of giving and never receiving. Your mentality of who you are and what you can do is likely underdeveloped because your mental capacity has never been adequately challenged, nurtured, or developed.

The potential within you is vast, but it requires the right kind of effort, discipline, and awareness to break through the barriers of awkwardness, self-doubt, and insecurity. Just as physical strength is built through consistent effort and overcoming resistance, mental strength comes from actively engaging with challenges that stretch your thinking and push your boundaries. You are capable of far more than you realize, but only if you start developing your mental capacity with the same focus you would train any other skill. It is late in the game; you are tired; everyone around you is either too immature or tired; hell, we are all tired.

So, let's rip into this illusion.

I want you to see this book as an exploration of the cycles of giving and receiving love, the invisible wounds left by trauma, and the delicate journey toward balance and healing. Through personal reflections and hard-earned wisdom, it uncovers how past pain shapes our ability to connect, trust, and be vulnerable. It delves into the struggles of those of us who loved too much, given too freely, or built walls too high to let love in. Blending lived experience with the insights gained from working with women and couples, it offers a story and a guide that illuminates the patterns we repeat, the lessons we learn, and the steps we must take to reclaim love on our terms.

Anticipating the Pain Instead of Accepting the Love, we'll interweave your journey with themes of trauma, relationship dynamics, and healing to help you connect my stories with yours while offering practical and emotional guidance.

Chapter 1: Anticipating The Pain

You knew deep down that the person was going to disappoint you. You might not have known precisely when or how it would happen, but that feeling was there—a warning you had come to recognize. It was like a tolerable roommate, an annoying sibling, or a disheartening neighborhood. It felt familiar. Love makes you hold on and hope, even while preparing for a fall. When it finally happened, it hurt because of their actions and because you allowed yourself to believe this time would be different. Now you're left feeling angry, but the frustration is directed at yourself for letting it happen again.

A nticipating pain can be particularly agonizing. It creates a cycle of anxiety. You dread that it amplifies the experience of suffering. When you know something painful is coming, your mind races through scenarios, amplifying fears and worries. This mental preparation usually proves to be more tormenting than the pain itself. For instance, it's the thoughts in your head as you go from class to class, worrying about the spanking your parents promised you when you get home from school. It's that split second of a static electric shock you feel when reaching for the doorknob in winter. It's also that knot in your stomach when you muster the courage to approach someone more attractive than you, only for them to turn you away. The waiting period can stretch out time, making every second feel like an eternity. It's not just the threat of emotional pain that's difficult; it's the emotional weight of betrayal, loss, disappointment, or helplessness that comes with expectation. This mental rehearsal of pain can poison your thoughts and distort your reality, making you feel trapped in your mind or reality. When the actual pain eventually arrives, it often carries the additional burden of all that anticipation, hitting you with double the force—once through fear and once through the experience. The culmination of these emotions and expectations can leave the mind and body in a heightened state of distress, making the anticipation of pain one of the most challenging aspects to endure.

Allow me to reiterate that for most of my life, I've been the giver in relationships—the one who pours out love, energy, patience, and understanding but rarely receives the same in return. I convinced myself it was enough to make the other person happy, even if it meant neglecting my needs. But one day, I asked myself: *What about me?*

They say that unresolved trauma keeps us stuck emotionally and socially at the age we were when the pain occurred. If you were nine, twenty-two, or fifty-five years old when the trauma occurred, you are likely still stuck at that age mentally. I brushed this idea aside for years, but now I see it can be true. This realization has been a significant step in my journey towards self-awareness and healing. Recognizing the importance of self-awareness and healing can make us feel validated and understood in our struggles. It's a reassurance that we're not alone in this journey and that there is a path to healing and growth.

With Mr. Opportunity (a man I am giving the opportunity), I find myself acting like a giddy teenager experiencing her first love—blushing, fumbling, and unsure of myself—despite being older than him. Mr. Opportunity is a man who has come into my life at a time when I was not expecting love. He has been a great man, helping me through many challenges and being everything, I need. I am grateful for his presence and the love he offers, but it also brings up much emotional turmoil.

People often come to me for advice about their relationships. Wives call, venting about their husbands, and even some men tell their partners, "Call Andrea—she'll help you see what I'm saying." I've become the person others turn to for clarity and guidance. But now, faced with the possibility of being loved for who I am—truly loved, without strings or expectations—I find myself frozen. I try not to think about it or to not lean in that direction. I have the freedom to think about it in any other way. I want to feel the love and feel loved. Instead of welcoming love, I anticipate pain. Instead of opening my heart, I brace for impact. I do it every time.

It's exhausting. I'm tired of this roller coaster ride. I'm weary of trying to fill the void by being so loving and constantly needing to love others, convincing myself that their happiness is enough for me. It's not. It never has.

I am standing at a crossroads: Should I continue anticipating the pain, or should I dare to accept the love? I know I don't hate myself; my mother ensured that, and I have held onto this confidence. But there's always a "But!" This internal conflict is a constant companion, a battle between my past and potential for a different future. It takes courage to consider a different future, but it's a courage we all possess, waiting to be ignited. If we take that first step, courage can lead us to a life filled with love and joy. It's the kind of courage that makes us feel strong and capable, ready to face whatever comes our way.

Anticipating pain is a learned behavior and an instinctive response that varies depending on your context. At its core, it functions as a survival mechanism, hardwired into the brain through evolution. The body instinctively prepares for harm—flinching before touching something hot or bracing for impact before a fall. This anticipation of physical or emotional pain triggers a series of responses in the brain and body, preparing us to avoid or endure the impending harm. The amygdala, the brain's fear center, controls this reflexive reaction, which helps detect threats and trigger protective responses. This biological anticipation of pain has been essential for survival, enabling humans to avoid life-threatening situations and physical harm.

Beyond these automatic responses, the emotional and mental anticipation of pain is mainly learned. Past experiences significantly shape how individuals expect and respond to suffering, affecting their ability to trust, love, and take risks. For instance, if someone has experienced repeated rejection, betrayal, or trauma, their brain may begin to expect similar pain in the future. This learned anticipation can lead to defensive behaviors, such as avoiding deep relationships, fearing failure, or withdrawing from opportunities that feel too vulnerable. In some cases, individuals might even preemptively conclude that every man will break their heart.

Family and upbringing play a significant role in shaping a child's emotional responses. A child raised in an unstable or critical environment may view emotional pain as unavoidable, often bracing for it even before it occurs. Similar to a situation where a parent prepares to punish a child, every time the parent draws back to strike, the child instinctively hunches as if caught in a dance of anticipation with the parent.

A cycle of fear is created; it's expected in the relationship. Having learned to expect harm, the child reflexively reacts before the blow lands—flinching, hunching, or recoiling in anticipation. A "dance" suggests a repeated, almost choreographed interaction between the parent and child, where one's action triggers the other's reaction in a tragic, conditioned pattern. Each time the parent raises a hand to strike, the child instinctively hunches— flinching before the blow even lands. It's a reflex born not just from past pain but from the expectation of it, a rhythm between them. In this unspoken dance, the child moves to the beat of fear, anticipating hurt before it happens, as if bracing could soften the impact. It doesn't. The pain is the pain.

This dynamic can manifest emotionally rather than physically in a couple's relationship. If one partner has been repeatedly criticized, dismissed, or hurt through words, actions, or neglect, they may start to anticipate disappointment even before it happens. Like the child who instinctively hunches before a blow, a partner in an unhealthy relationship might flinch or become emotional at a specific tone of voice and withdraw before a discussion or argument begins. You assume rejection or reflections before giving love a chance.

Over time, this creates a cycle: one person's past wounds shape their reactions, influencing the other person's behavior and reinforcing patterns of distance, fear, or miscommunication. Instead of true intimacy, the relationship becomes a careful, defensive dance, each person moving to avoid the next expected wound rather than stepping toward love, even avoiding each other.

Similarly, societal and cultural influences can reinforce specific attitudes toward pain. In environments where vulnerability is perceived as weakness, individuals often learn to suppress their struggles, expecting hardship yet never expressing their feelings.

Since much of the anticipation of emotional pain is learned, it can also be unlearned.

The first step is recognizing that not every situation will lead to suffering. Challenging negative thought patterns, distinguishing past wounds from present realities, and building self-awareness can help break the cycle. Overcoming deeply ingrained fears requires conscious effort, patience, and, in some cases, professional support. It is an ongoing process, trust me. While pain is an unavoidable part of life, living in constant anticipation of it is not. By shifting focus from fear to possibility, you free yourself from expected suffering and open the door to healing and connection.

Unlearning the Anticipation of Pain

Most of us will struggle to break free from this cycle because it becomes deeply ingrained in our sense of self and relationships.

Breaking free requires more than just leaving; it demands unlearning, healing, and rebuilding. And that can feel overwhelming when you've spent a lifetime anticipating the pain instead of accepting the love.

1. **Familiarity Feels Safe:** Even if it's painful, a toxic dynamic can feel more predictable and comfortable than the unknown. Many of you mistake familiarity for love, clinging to what you know rather than risking something new or someone new.

2. **Emotional Conditioning:** Just like the child who instinctively hunches, those of you in these relationships develop automatic responses to protect themselves. Over time, you stop questioning the pattern and accept it as usual. Even convincing others, "Whatever doesn't break you will make you stronger." This is not always true.

3. **Fear of Abandonment or Loss**: Even if the relationship is unhealthy, leaving means facing loneliness, rejection, or the fear that no one else will love you. This fear can be more powerful than the pain of staying.

4. **Low Self-Worth**: When you have been conditioned to believe you are unworthy of love, respect, or kindness, you may not even recognize that you deserve better. You might even blame yourself for the toxic dynamic.

5. **Hope for Change**: Many of you will hold on to the idea that the partner or family member will eventually change, that love will "fix" things, or that if you try harder, you can make the relationship work. This hope keeps you trapped.

6. **Cultural and Societal Pressures**: Family expectations, religious beliefs, financial dependence, or societal stigma around failed relationships can make leaving seem impossible. Some of you can leave and afford to be on your own, but not at the level of luxury you have now. So, you stay for a better material life or a lifestyle you can't afford.

7. **Fear of Confronting Pain**: Walking away means facing the root of the pain, often childhood wounds or long-buried trauma. Many of you aren't ready to do that work, so you stay in the cycle because it keeps deeper wounds hidden. If I don't acknowledge it, it doesn't exist.

Breaking free from the cycle of anticipating pain is not about denying that pain exists; it's about reclaiming the present instead of living in fear of the future. Since much of emotional pain anticipation is learned, it can be unlearned, but it requires a strong conscious effort, self-awareness, and a willingness to challenge deeply ingrained patterns. It starts with recognizing that not every situation will lead to suffering, that past wounds do not have to dictate future experiences, and that pain, while inevitable, does not have to be lived in advance. Waiting for it, expecting it, anticipating it is lived in advance.

One of the first steps is challenging the mind's automatic responses. When pain has been a constant teacher, the brain begins to expect it, often misreading neutral or even positive situations as threats. A simple miscommunication in a relationship may feel like the beginning of abandonment. A new opportunity at work may seem like a setup for failure. The key is to pause and question these thoughts: Is this fear based on what is happening, or is it a projection of past wounds?

Learning to separate past pain from present reality is a decisive step toward breaking the cycle.

Reframing vulnerability as a strength is another critical shift. Many people anticipate pain because they see emotional exposure as dangerous. If they were hurt after opening up in the past, they may believe the only way to stay safe is to remain guarded. But real connection, growth, and healing only happen when walls come down. Instead of seeing vulnerability as a risk, it can be reframed as a courageous act that makes life richer rather than more dangerous. And, yes, that need for excitement or being like everyone else can drive it that much more.

Mindfulness and grounding techniques help rewire your response to anticipated pain. Fear pulls people out of the present, making them relive past wounds or worry about future suffering. Practicing mindfulness can break this cycle through meditation, deep breathing, or simply focusing on the current moment. It's simple but effective. When the mind starts racing toward pain that hasn't yet arrived, grounding techniques bring it back to reality, reminding the body and brain that, at this moment, everything is okay.

Unlearning the anticipation of pain is not about pretending life will always be easy. It is about recognizing that pain can be faced when it comes, and it can be faced when it arrives without allowing it to take over before it has a chance to happen. It is about reclaiming joy, presence, and connection and refusing to let fear steal the moments that pain has not yet touched.

I know pain is inevitable, but the waiting, the knowing, the anticipating is often worse than the wound itself. It lingers like a shadow, stretching moments into eternity, tightening its grip with every uncertain breath. The mind fixates, creating endless scenarios of suffering, rehearsing each possible heartbreak, rejection, or failure before it even arrives. The body reacts like the pain is already here: tense muscles, shallow breaths, and a racing heart. And so, long before the actual moment of hurt, we have already lived it a thousand times in our heads.

Anticipating pain is not just a defense mechanism; it becomes a way of life. It will shape the way we love, the way we connect, the way we build or destroy the spaces around us. We tiptoe through relationships, bracing for disappointment. We silence ourselves at work, fearing rejection. We pull away from family, expecting misunderstanding. In trying to avoid pain, we become trapped in a constant state of suffering, one that exists only in our minds but feels just as accurate, real, and surreal.

Rebuilding trust in oneself, in others, and life is essential. Many who anticipate pain have lost faith in navigating difficult moments. However, healing does not come from avoiding all pain but from trusting that you will move forward no matter what happens. Learning to trust again, step by step, allows you to move forward without constantly bracing for impact.

Being Mindful is Best

Being mindful means being fully present and aware of your thoughts, emotions, and surroundings without reacting impulsively. It involves recognizing patterns in your behavior, feelings, or interactions and understanding how they impact you and others.

When it comes to change, mindfulness enables you to notice when something is happening—or about to happen—that requires adjustment. For example, if you tend to become defensive in specific conversations, mindfulness allows you to catch that reaction before it escalates. Instead of automatically responding, you can pause, reflect, and choose a different approach.

It functions like an internal alarm system that alerts you to moments where growth is possible. The key is to observe without judgment, accept what is, and make intentional choices to shift behaviors that no longer serve you.

Family: The Ghosts of Past Wounds

Family should be a place of comfort, a safe environment, and a trusting place, but for many, it is where the first wounds are inflicted. A child raised in instability becomes an adult who never fully trusts closeness, always waiting for love to be withdrawn. A partner or parent who carried their unhealed pain may have passed it on in sharp words, in cold silences, in expectations too heavy for a child to bear. These cycles continue, shaping generations to come, teaching us to expect pain even in the safest spaces, that no place is secure.

In some families, pain is delivered through abandonment, addiction, or affliction. It is silent but ever-present, woven into the fabric of relationships through unspoken tension and unresolved issues. The anticipation of hurt keeps people from reconciling, expressing love freely, and healing what has been broken. Instead of confronting the past, you live in its shadow, expecting history to repeat itself. Guess what? It will happen every time you wish.

Breaking Free with Ambition: The Fear of Failing Before We Begin

Anticipating pain doesn't just affect relationships. It infiltrates mentalities, careers, ambitions, and self-worth. The fear of rejection can silence your voice long before you speak. Doubt convinces people to settle for less than they deserve or want. The weight of past failures makes every new opportunity feel like a risk too significant to take.

Some stay in toxic work environments, believing mistreatment is inevitable and expected, and sadly, they grow to appreciate it. Others hold back everything from feelings to ideas, fearing ridicule or dismissal. Talented people remain unseen, unheard, or feel unwanted, not because they lack ability but because they have already convinced themselves they will fail. The anticipation of failure becomes more paralyzing than failure itself. And so, success is not lost in defeat. It is lost in never trying (never attempting). You can become numb to this feeling. You can be broken so bad that it feels normal; that pain feels normal. It feels familiar.

Work and ambition should stem from a place of passion, not fear. When you stop anticipating failure, you will begin to realize your potential. For many of us, the fear of failure doesn't just appear when we take risks; it can prevent us from starting in the first place. We hesitate, overthink, or convince ourselves to avoid opportunities before taking the first step. But why?

1. **Fear of Judgment**: You aren't just afraid of failing; you fear being seen as failures. The prospect of looking incompetent, disappointing others, or confirming your doubts can make you hesitate.

2. **Internalized Expectations**: Many of you will bear the burden of expectations from family, society, or ourselves. If you have been taught that success equates to worth, then failure can feel like confirmation that you are not enough.

3. **Past Wounds**: If you've experienced criticism, dismissal, or feelings of inadequacy, you might believe that failure will only reinforce those negative beliefs. You may think, "Why try if I'll just prove them right?"

4. **Perfectionism as a Defense Mechanism**: Perfectionism isn't about high standards; it's a desire for control. If you can't guarantee success, you may choose not to try, avoiding failure and the discomfort of not measuring up.

Breaking Free: The Fear of Failing Before Beginning

1. **Redefine Failure**: Failure isn't the opposite of success; it's part of the journey. Every misstep offers opportunities for growth, clarity, and resilience. No one who succeeds has done so without facing some levels or stages of failure.

2. **Shift the Focus to Learning:** Instead of asking, "What if I fail?" ask, "What will I learn?" Growth occurs through action, not overthinking.

3. **Take Small, Imperfect Steps:** Fear thrives on hesitation. Taking action—any action—breaks this cycle. Start small, embrace imperfection, and gradually build your confidence.

4. **Detach Your Worth from Outcomes:** Your success or failure does not determine your value. It's defined by your willingness to keep moving onward.

5. **Normalize Discomfort**: Fear isn't a signal to stop; it indicates that you're stretching beyond your comfort zone. Instead of waiting for fear to disappear, learn to move forward despite it. Fear can make you better prepared.

Love & Relationships: Preparing for Heartbreak Before it Happens

Love is no longer a sanctuary for those who have been:

1. **Habitually Hurt**: Experiencing ongoing emotional pain due to repeated toxic behaviors.
2. **Always Abandoned**: Consistently feeling left behind or unsupported in relationships.
3. **Deeply Disappointed**: Facing repeated letdowns from someone you trusted or relied on.
4. **Repeatedly Let Down**: Being promised love, change, or commitment but constantly seeing those promises broken.
5. **Severely Betrayed:** Suffering a significant violation of trust, such as infidelity or deception.
6. **Constantly Neglected**: Feeling unseen, unheard, or emotionally starved in a relationship.

7. **Persistently Rejected**: Continuously feeling unwanted, whether in love, communication, or intimacy.

8. **Endlessly Disregarded**: Your emotions, needs, or concerns are consistently dismissed.

9. **Unfairly Mistreated**: Facing undeserved criticism, control, or emotional abuse.

10. **Regularly Overlooked**: Feeling unimportant in the relationship, as if your presence doesn't matter.

11. **Harshly Judged**: Experiencing excessive criticism or unrealistic expectations from a partner.

12. **Cruelly Deceived**: Being lied to or manipulated in ways that damage trust.

13. **Utterly Forsaken**: Feeling completely abandoned emotionally, even if the person is physically present.

14. **Frequently Unappreciated**: Having your efforts and love taken for granted.

15. **Coldly Ignored**: Experiencing the silent treatment or emotional distance as a form of control or neglect.

16. **Unjustly Blamed**: Being accused of problems or faults in the relationship that are not you're doing.

17. **Painfully Excluded**: Feeling left out of important moments, decisions, or emotional connections.

18. **Abruptly Dismissed**: Having your concerns, boundaries, or feelings brushed off without consideration.

19. **Hopelessly Deserted**: Feeling emotionally or physically abandoned when you need support the most.

20. **Silently Suffering**: Enduring pain or loneliness in a relationship without expression, often out of fear or exhaustion.

It is a fight. It is a battlefield. It is war.

Every new connection is met with hesitation; every kind word is dissected for hidden meaning, and a whisper of doubt follows every moment of closeness. Will they leave? Will they change? Will they cheat? Will they cheat again? Will I be enough? Instead of fully experiencing love, we monitor it, searching for the earliest signs of collapse. Sometimes, many times, often we provoke it. Yes, we prepare for heartbreak before it happens, sometimes so much that we cause it ourselves. "Sick of waiting, I might as well get it over with. I will say or do something knowing it's going to end. At least that's better than suffering.

Some of you build walls too high for love to reach; others keep on the move, believing distance is safer than vulnerability. Many of you grip too tightly, mistaking control for security, suffocating what you wish to protect. The anticipation of pain turns love into something to fear rather than cherish. Ultimately, we don't lose love because someone leaves; we lose it because we never fully allowed ourselves to experience it.

Breaking Free: Living Without Bracing for Impact

Breaking free doesn't mean you'll never feel fear again. It means no longer allowing that fear to control your ability to love and be loved. It means standing in the present instead of recoiling from the past. The anticipation of pain can sometimes be worse than the pain itself. When we expect hurt, betrayal, or disappointment, we guard ourselves before anything happens. In doing so, we rob ourselves of the present moment—of joy, love, and connection—because we're so focused on what might go wrong. It's like living in the shadow of a storm that may never come. The fear of suffering becomes it's kind of suffering, preventing us from fully experiencing the good already in our lives. In relationships, this can manifest as pushing people away, doubting their kindness, or bracing for rejection before it occurs. The real thief isn't always the pain itself; it's our fear of it. Recognizing this can help us reclaim our joy, even in uncertain moments.

What if we allowed ourselves to love fully instead of bracing for heartbreak? Instead of expecting rejection, we could step into our true power and capabilities. Rather than preparing for the worst, embrace the possibility of something better.

Living without the constant need to brace for emotional impact is possible, but it requires conscious effort, self-awareness, a willingness to change the patterns that have shaped your relationships, and mindfulness.

1. **Recognizing the Pattern**: Breaking free from something means recognizing you've been living in a cycle of anticipation—flinching emotionally, expecting rejection, or preparing for the worst in love. Pay attention to when you instinctively shut down, apologize excessively, or withdraw before anything happens.

2. **Understanding Where it Comes From (Ask yourself)**: Why do I brace for impact? These behaviors often stem from past wounds—such as childhood experiences, previous relationships, or deep-seated fears of abandonment. Recognizing the source helps you separate old pain from your present reality.

3. **Rewiring Your Response**: Rather than reacting out of fear, practice responding with intention. When you notice yourself expecting hurt, pause and ask: Is this fear based on the present

moment or my past? Learning to self-soothe and reassure yourself during these moments is crucial.

4. **Allowing Yourself to Receive Love:** Many of you keep love at arm's length because you don't trust it. Practice allowing kindness, affection, and support into your life without questioning whether you "deserve" it or worrying about when it might disappear.

5. **Setting Boundaries**: Breaking free doesn't only involve leaving toxic relationships; it also means creating space for healthier dynamics. Establish boundaries that protect your peace, and don't apologize for needing safety, respect, and emotional security.

6. **Healing Your Nervous System**: When you've lived in a state of emotional bracing for too long, your body and mind can remain on high alert. Activities like therapy, mindfulness, deep breathing, and even physical movement (such as yoga or walking) can help retrain your nervous system to relax and feel safe in love. Create a healthier diet.

7. **Relearning Trust—In Yourself and Others**: Trust isn't about believing no one will ever hurt you; it's about knowing you will handle it if they do. Trusting yourself means recognizing red flags, honoring your needs, and knowing when to walk away. This frees you from the need to brace for impact constantly.

Pain will come, that is certain. But to live in constant anticipation of it is to suffer twice, once in fear and once in reality. The challenge is not to avoid pain but to stop giving it space in moments it has not yet touched. We must recognize that the walls we build to keep it out also keep out love, joy, and connection. Just like a fort keeps the enemy out, it also keeps the feared in.

The actual test is not whether we can avoid pain but whether we can face life without flinching, without retreating, without letting the fear of suffering become suffering itself.

Because in the end, the worst kind of pain is the one we never had to endure but lived through anyway.

Standard Powers vs. Superpowers

Powers that differ in their scale to impact others. Everyone can achieve standard power through practice and persistence, while superpower represents the extraordinary expansion of what seems possible.

Standard power refers to the abilities and strengths within your everyday limits, whether physical, mental, emotional, or social. It includes intelligence, resilience, leadership, and influence. A strong work ethic, the ability to inspire others, and even physical endurance are examples of your standard power. You develop these skills and qualities through effort, experience, and discipline.

A superpower goes beyond the ordinary. Your extraordinary abilities, like super strength, extreme patience, telekinesis, or focus, defy natural limits. A superpower is your exceptional talent or ability that sets you apart from others. It is your emotional intelligence, extreme creativity, or an uncanny ability to lead and adapt.

Chapter 2: The Roller Coaster

You find yourself more prepared for the challenges of love than ready to embrace it. You've convinced yourself that love is something to endure, judged by how well you survive the lows rather than how freely you accept the highs. When you anticipate pain more than welcoming joy, you grapple with a deeper issue. Like a roller coaster, it's the same cycle: waiting for the next drop (subsequent disappointment) and the same curves (reason to guard your heart). Love isn't supposed to be something you prepare to lose. It isn't meant to be a ride you cling to out of fear. It's not a roller coaster.

Allow me to set the scene for you. It's a warm, sunny afternoon at the fairground. My friends and I, a group of teenagers, walk toward the roller coaster, chatting and laughing. So, you have us girls and a few new guys, and one of them is Kenny. He is the "new-new" guy on the street.

As a teenager in a town with a fair that ran year-round, the roller coaster was a familiar and thrilling part of our routine. Just like you might have familiar and exciting experiences, we'd spend the day at the fairgrounds, the highlight, the main event always being the roller coaster, a ride we all knew so well. It was like an old friend, always there to provide a rush of excitement, a feeling I'm sure many of you can relate to.

The roller coaster was an emotional buffet, a thrill we eagerly anticipated. After paying to board the cart, it was a task within itself to know who you would sit next to. You braced yourself for all the emotions you knew were coming. We often talked and laughed as the cart slowly moved along the trail. Strapped securely in place, our hearts beat faster with anticipation of something exciting going to happen. We'd been on this ride a hundred times, but still, there was anticipation. The first hill to climb over is always the smallest; it's like an emotional tease. You close your eyes and brace yourself as you reach the top. The drop on the other side is gut-wrenching. You laugh it off and say, "Oh, it wasn't that bad". This anticipation and thrill are something I'm sure many of you have experienced on a roller coaster ride.

Some scream fear, a few will cry, but everyone yells as the cart descends with vigor, then a quick jerk left and another right. As you gear up for another jerk, you feel smoothness, as though all is claimed. When you get your breath on the straight track, you are jerked back up and carried to another assault on your senses. The experience is repetitive, just like the roller coaster ride. It mirrors the repetitive, sometimes painful, and often emotionally draining nature of the relationships I would later experience. There is nothing that hasn't been cleaned from these carts. People have lost shoes, coins, spit, vomit, tears, pee, and even food that they hide. As you make your final descent from the largest hill, you feel a sense of longing because you know it has to end. We've been here so many times, but the sensations still come. You then have to decide if you will pay the price and go another round, beg the conductor to do it again or get off the ride because today, you don't feel like taking your emotions in the same circles, jerks, or route.

Looking back, I realize the roller coaster was more than a ride. It was the beginning of a journey towards understanding dysfunctional relationships. The roller coaster, or at least the experience of it, was a metaphor for the relationships I would later find myself in. Like the roller coaster, these relationships were fun, thrilling, and unpredictable, with moments of fear and excitement. They were repetitive, sometimes painful, and often left me feeling like I was on an emotional roller coaster. The roller coaster's ups and downs, twists and turns, and moments of anticipation and fear mirrored these relationships' emotional journey. This emotional journey is something I'm sure many of you can relate to in your relationships.

It was another beautiful sunny day, and we walked around the fairgrounds. This day felt different because some new guys went with us on the street. I had my eyes on the oldest. His smile always lit up the room. It was a contagious type of smile, and when you see him smiling, no matter how you are feeling, you start smiling, too. He was gentle and kind. Not like the other boys who would give a compliment and then take it back with, "You would be prettier if you'd just lose some weight." Yet, I dared not let anyone other than my best friend know I liked him. If anyone else knew it would become jokes, teasing, and making fun, they would laugh at me.

I was beyond shy, always walking a few steps behind the others. I was always making myself needed and ready to share whatever money I had. My mother always made sure I had enough. She made sure I never had to ask anyone for anything. This gave me a status. I was the girl who always had extra funds. But this day went so differently from all the other days. This was the day a handsome boy, Kenny, laughed and joked with me like I was special. I have watched it so many times with my friends. At first, it didn't feel normal. I was anticipating something horrible. He even teased me like I had seen happen to other girls. The teasing the popular girls get. I didn't want to think too much of it. I was afraid that it was superficial. I feared that it would end with me being the butt of a joke.

For some reason, on this day, I enjoyed the moment. Thoughts came, but somehow, I recognized it as an honest, sincere, authentic engagement. Recognizing genuine engagement is a key step in understanding and valuing healthy relationships. Kenny was not looting a joke at my expense. Kenny was a boy who liked a girl. And that girl was me, being a girl. Kenny's actions and genuine engagement with me were key lessons in understanding and valuing healthy relationships.

Then, it was time to go over to the roller coaster.

I was my usual self and walked behind the crew and smiled as they had fun. It made me happy to see other people happy even if I wasn't. At least, that is how I remember it. As we were about to board the cart, something stranger than ever happened. This was going to shake up the entire group. Kenny intentionally made his way to the cart I was in. Immediately, the crew couldn't help themselves. They started raining jokes and poking fun. I heard the jokes, but I dared not say no. I slid over and let him enter. I closed my eyes because I wanted to make sure I was ready for the ride. I also closed my eyes because Kenny was sitting next to me. I did as I had learned to do and prayed this would not end badly. "Please God..." To my surprise, as the cart rose, so were his arms. I could see he was going to put his arms around me. At that moment, I forgot all about the hill with snatches, turns, and jerks that were coming. I wasn't sure what to do. This was new. I had no plan for this. I had seen guys make these moves on girls in the movies. I have seen what others do in the carts, but this was me. This was the girl who hid in the shadows of her pretty friends. I was the girl who intentionally walked a few steps behind. For some reason, the sensations passed. I didn't feel fear. So, I smiled and laughed like I always had this happen.

Every climb, descent, jerk, and turn felt different this time. Not unfamiliarly different, just different. He leaned over and kissed me as the ride was coming to a close. Me, Andrea, the girl who had watched him since he moved in and wondered what it would be like to hold his hand. To have his arms around me. What kissing him would feel like. In all my awkwardness, I allowed the kiss. I had no idea what would happen when we got off the ride. All I could think about was if he would kiss me again, and I wanted to stay on and do it again. Let me be honest: if I recall correctly, we rode it several times.

When we did get off, it was like it never happened. He was still super friendly to me. Until his dying day, well into his 40s, he was always a champion and protector for me and others. Some guys are just good people.

When my mother couldn't maintain her yard, Kenny would do it for her. He was unique; it was who he was. And this in itself is special. Kenny's normal powers are many other people's superpowers.

Unfortunately, this is not a fairytale. Nothing more came from the kiss. Maybe he just knew I needed attention at the time. Maybe he needed attention. I don't know. I will likely never know. I was too shy ever to ask.

Over the years, as I've spoken to thousands of people, I've realized that many relationships are much like that roller coaster ride from my childhood. There's the initial excitement, the thrill of something new, the anticipation of what's to come. Then, the first drop, sometimes small, sometimes gut-wrenching, followed by the climb back up, the brief moments of peace before another sharp turn or unexpected fall. Some relationships, like roller coasters, are full of highs and lows, ups and downs, leaving us breathless, exhilarated, or even terrified. And yet, we still get on; we stay on, gripping tightly, convincing ourselves that the good moments make the tough one's worth it. We scream, laugh, and brace for impact, knowing deep down that the ride never changes. But the longer we stay on, the more we miss what lies beyond the rest of the park, the many other rides and excitements, the quiet joys, the steady, simple pleasures that don't come with a sudden drop. The question isn't whether the roller coaster will keep going in circles or take the same routes as it always does. The real question is: When do we decide to step off? What does that feel like?

Breaking Free from the Relationship Roller Coaster to Recognize the Pattern

The first step in change is acknowledging the cycle. When your relationships consistently follow the same highs and lows, intense excitement followed by emotional turmoil, it's time to step back and assess. Are you holding on because of absolute happiness? Are you staying because the ups temporarily make up for the downs? Identifying patterns allows you to see what it is: a cycle that will keep repeating unless you choose to get off that ride.

Shift Your Perspective on Love

Love should not be something you endure, nor should it leave you constantly bracing for the next drop. A healthy relationship is not about how well you can survive the turbulence but how safe and valued you feel. It is a mutual responsibility for two people to make each other feel valued. If you anticipate pain more than embracing love, the relationship is not serving your emotional well-being. True love offers consistency, mutuality, and fairness, not temporary highs between inevitable lows.

Set Boundaries and Prioritize Your Emotional Need

Stepping off the ride means redefining what you will and won't accept in a relationship. This requires setting clear boundaries for yourself and others. Ask yourself: What do I genuinely need in "this" relationship? What behaviors am I no longer willing to tolerate? When prioritizing your emotional well-being, you naturally create space for healthier, more fulfilling connections. "This" is important because it shifts the focus from general relationship ideals to your specific situation. It forces you to reflect on your current or past relationship patterns and evaluate what is serving you versus harming you.

By asking, "What do I genuinely need in this" relationship?" you personalize the process, making it more intentional and actionable rather than theoretical.

Boundaries are not just about saying "no" to others. They are about saying" yes" to yourself. Without a clear understanding of boundaries, you will continue accepting behaviors that drain, confuse, or make you feel unworthy of the love you truly deserve. Prioritizing your emotional well-being is key because when you set boundaries, you communicate your needs, values, and expectations. This protects your mental and emotional health and attracts relationships that align with your self-worth.

Defining what you will and won't accept can be viewed as selfish, but it is also the foundation for healthier, more fulfilling connections. Without it, you risk staying on the roller coaster, repeating the same cycles, and mistaking emotional highs and lows for real love.

Embrace Discomfort and Trust the Process

Leaving a familiar pattern, no matter how unhealthy, can feel unsettling. You will second-guess yourself, fear the unknown, or wonder if you're making the right choice. But growth often comes with discomfort. Trust that stepping off the emotional roller coaster leads you to relationships that offer peace, stability, and genuine happiness.

What Else is People Doing Out There

Imagine the fairground beyond the roller coaster—new experiences, new connections, new opportunities for joy—a place intended to make you happy, not show unhappiness. When we step outside traditional Western narratives, we discover a world of diverse and innovative approaches to healing and cultivating relationships. Around the globe, people blend ancient wisdom with modern insights to create balanced and authentic partnerships. For instance, in Brazil, some people turn to spiritual rituals—sometimes including sorcery—to mend heartbreak and forge stronger bonds, reflecting a cultural blend of mysticism and healing. In Hawaii, the ancient practice of "Ho'oponopono" focuses on forgiveness and reconciliation to clear emotional residue and restore balance. Similarly, among the Tumbuka people of Malawi, Tanzania, and Zambia, the Vimbuza healing dance creates a trance-like state through music and movement, helping participants release negative energy and reconnect with their community.

Many modern seekers combine practices like Ayahuasca ceremonies—which are used to gain clarity and emotional release—with mindfulness and therapy to move past relationship pain. In other regions, acupuncture has been embraced as a tool to stimulate the release of endorphins and break the cycle of emotional distress.

After gathering insights, engage in cross-cultural exchanges by discussing these practices with people from different backgrounds. This broadens your perspective and helps you appreciate the cultural context behind each healing method, enriching your journey.

Finally, integrate what resonates with you into a personalized healing plan. Combine modern therapy with a practice or ritual that feels right for you—whether a structured forgiveness ritual like "Ho'oponopono," a communal healing dance, or adopting a more mindful, holistic approach to your relationships. This fusion can help you move away from traditional patterns that no longer serve you, embracing a more balanced, globally inspired way of connecting.

Chapter 3: The Crossroads

At a certain point in our lives, we all face a crucial decision: continue to anticipate pain or open ourselves to love. This crossroads is a pivotal moment in life; Road 1: a choice between the comfort of familiar patterns; Road 2. the safety and security provided; Road 3: the discomfort of healing; and Road 4: where love is given and received to move forward. No path is easy. No road is smooth. But we must break the cycle, reclaim our worth, and embrace love without fear. At some point, all the roads cross each other; that's the crossroad.

Now, I'm faced with something unfamiliar: the possibility of being on the receiving end of love, of being seen, valued, and cherished for who I am. Instead of celebrating this, I find myself bracing for the inevitable heartbreak, the weight of my struggles pressing down on me. I spent so long anticipating the pain that I didn't know how to accept the love. I don't know how, though I know how to tell others to do it. My advice works for them. It scares the living heebie-jeebies out of me.

I've walked the path of vulnerability and trust, and I want you to know I understand. Your emotions are valid, and you're not alone in this journey. It's okay to feel like you do; we all navigate this path. I want to emphasize that you're not alone in this struggle with vulnerability and trust. We're in this together.

This is the crossroads I find myself at now. I keep repeating the same patterns. It may be because I don't know how to break my cycle, I am comfortable with the cycle, or loving others to distract me from myself, from my many needs. So, I anticipate the hurt even when love is offered. Is it more comfortable and familiar than letting someone in? It's a stark reminder of the weight of our habits and the urgent need for change, the pressing necessity for personal growth. It's essential to reflect on your patterns and habits and consider how they might affect your relationships and personal growth. I am worthy of receiving the same love that I give. The love, the much-needed love, a valuable love I have freely given to others? It's about finding the balance between giving and receiving, and I'm on a journey to discover my equilibrium. Remember, personal growth is a journey, not a destination. It's about the steps we take, the lessons we learn, and the person we become.

Let this journey inspire you to invest in your personal growth, which can lead to a more fulfilling life. Self-reflection has been a crucial part of my journey, and I encourage you to engage in your introspective journey as a key part of your personal growth. Embrace self-reflection and introspection in your journey of personal growth. Self-reflection is a powerful tool for personal development. It allows you to understand your strengths and weaknesses, identify areas for improvement, and make conscious decisions to change and grow.

These decisions in my personal life also affect how I do business. It tampers with my abilities to be a professional. I don't want to do business alone; I prefer a partner. I don't want to continue going home to an empty house.

The phone rings, it's one of the many emotional cases I help. I remind them of, '...when you are not at your best, it will stop progress in family and business...' I noticed this for myself within a few minutes of Katrina, my assistant, showing up. This personal struggle with love and trust affects my professional relationships, making it difficult for me to engage in my work thoroughly. But it's also a reminder that personal growth is not just a personal matter; it's a powerful tool for professional success. It's a journey, but it's a journey worth taking, and it can significantly impact your professional life. Your personal growth is not just for you; it's for your career, relationships, and future. It's a powerful reminder that personal growth is not just a personal matter; it's essential for professional success. It's a journey, but it's a journey worth taking, and it can significantly impact your professional life. Remember, every step you take towards personal growth is a step towards a more fulfilling professional life. Let this inspire you to invest in your personal growth, which can lead to a more successful professional life.

Personal growth is not just about improving your personal life, but it also has a direct impact on your professional life. As I've learned, my struggles with love and trust have affected my ability to engage in my work thoroughly. By investing in your personal growth, you can become a more effective professional, build stronger relationships, and achieve tremendous success in your career. This connection between personal and professional growth is a key aspect of my journey, and I hope it can inspire you to consider the broader implications of your personal growth. There is hope for growth in your professional life.

Personal growth can enhance your professional life by improving your interpersonal skills, increasing your self-awareness, and boosting your resilience in the face of challenges.

The Seeds We Plant

There's something profoundly humbling about watching someone grow into their fullest potential, especially when you realize you had a hand planting the seeds of their growth long ago. These 'seeds' are small acts of kindness, like offering a listening ear during a tough time, words of encouragement, such as praising someone's unique talents, and lessons shared in passing, like sharing a personal experience that taught a valuable life lesson. For instance, I remember sharing my knowledge of overcoming a difficult breakup with a friend and how it inspired her to take control of her life. They are the nurturing elements we provide, often without realizing their potential impact. They may seem insignificant at the time, but years later, sometimes decades, they take root and bloom in ways we never imagined. These seeds could be as simple as a smile to a stranger, a compliment to a colleague, or advice to a friend.

She has blossomed. I never knew that seeds I planted years ago would show up nearly 30 years later in full fruition. It's a powerful reminder that our influence, whether intentional or not, doesn't just disappear. The way we treat people, the lessons we pass down, and the support we give can shape a person's path long after we've moved on. So many of us never see the results of the love and wisdom we pour into others. When we do, it's a powerful confirmation that every effort matters. It's beyond emotionally rewarding. It's a testament to the importance of our actions and the impact we can have on others.

This realization forces us to ask: What kind of seeds are we planting today? Are we sowing love, confidence, and resilience, or are we leaving behind doubt, fear, and insecurity? Just like a garden, what we invest in others, our children, friends, colleagues, and even strangers. Whether we are there to witness it or not, our words and actions have lasting power. It's a reminder of the importance of planting seeds of kindness because one day, when you least expect it, you may look up and see something beautiful blossoming before your eyes, reminding you that nothing given in love is ever wasted. This power is in your hands, and it's a responsibility we all share. You have the power to make a difference in someone's life, and it starts with the seeds you plant.

So, plant with intention. Offer kindness without expectation. Share wisdom without needing immediate proof of its impact. One day, when you least expect it, you may look up and see something beautiful blossoming before your eyes, reminding you that nothing given in love is ever wasted. Still, I have these questions because sometimes we invest in others to avoid investing in ourselves. It's important to remember that while investing in others is noble and rewarding, it's equally important to invest in ourselves. Self-investment is not selfish; it's necessary for personal growth and well-being. By taking care of ourselves, we can better serve and support others, and it's a crucial part of the journey to finding balance and happiness.

Remember, the most important investment you can make is in yourself. Don't forget to invest in yourself; it's your most important investment.

I met Katrina when she was 12 years of age. At the time, I was a licensed cosmetologist working in a salon. Katrina's mother was my client and came weekly to get her hair done. She spoke of her daughter, who didn't like to read. This was intriguing because of my passion for reading great books. When I met Katrina, she wanted her hair done weekly, just like her mother did. It was from there that we started what would become a lifelong relationship. Our friendship led to me proposing a unique deal. The deal was simple: I would do her hair if she read a book and wrote a simple report. She was initially hesitant, but she agreed. This 'deal' was not just about getting her to read, but it was a catalyst for her personal growth and development, and it strengthened our bond. This small act of kindness and encouragement, combined with her willingness to step out of her comfort zone, led to a significant transformation in her life. It's a testament to the lasting impact of our intentions and actions.

Fast forward to Katrina, now in her 40s, we crossed each other at a women's networking event in our local town. We spent some time catching up and reminiscing over the old days. A couple of weeks later, I got a call from Katrina. She said, "The Lord wanted her to help me with my ministry." This was a profound moment for me, as it reflected the impact of our relationship and the growth, we both experienced. It was a testament to the power of investing in others and its ripple effect on our lives.

The excitement ran through like a bolt of lightning. Not only was I grateful for the help, but it was Katrina. I remembered crying out for some assistance. An old saying is, "The squeaky wheel gets the oil." In this case, it was the intervention, blessing, and favor from God that I had been crying out for. I didn't expect the shift that needed to happen—the process of allowing and trusting someone into my space. I had to let someone into my dream. Katrina was not necessarily unknown to me, but she had become a proficient organizer. The little girl I had to bribe (strike a deal) to read is a trained and experienced organizer. An administrative force to be reckoned with. She is getting me right, straightening things out, and protecting me. I am ashamed that I didn't know how to receive all she had to offer initially. I had become stuck in my ways, resistant to change, and protective of my space.

I recall that this wasn't our first event together in Virginia. I started to remember how she operated. Katrina packed the things for each event. The first time, she shows up with her clipboard, a 3-page checklist, organized and ready to go. This blew my mind. Everything I needed, from clothes to the cleaners, packed bags, and an organized van, she did it. How could I know she was this professional, prepared, and persistent? I still dared to resist and push back against her. It was fear.

Here we are in Virginia. I'm the keynote speaker, and Katrina is managing my table. As I approached, I noticed she had pictures on her phone from previous events and images of the tables where I had rearranged things to suit my preferences. She never got upset when I changed things; instead, she took pictures to know exactly how to set it up next time. I didn't notice then, but it was as if she was prepared for my resistance.

I walk over as she finishes a sale and packs the boxes. Instinctively, I ask, did you add this, do that, remember this and that? I caught myself. I stopped. I could see the look on her face, and at that moment, I realized my mistake. My annoyance. My burden. She has already taken care of every detail. She takes pride in her work and ensures everything is right for the event, herself, and me. She was a professional, and I was scared. She isn't just doing a job; she's putting her heart into it. And more than anything, she wants to make me proud. This was not only overlooked by me but noticed by her. I felt this hurt me more than the fact I did it. She noticed it.

That day, the Lord told me he had sent the help I needed, and I was about to lose it because of my inadequacies. When Katrina came to my room to continue a great job, she was doing for the next day. She did what most people would think is small. She ensured I had eaten—another punch to my already growing walk of shame. I could no longer bear my guilt. I apologized to her for my attitude, untrusting behavior, and being a "micromanaging controlling tyrant." She is the humbled professional she is. She didn't say she accepted my apology. She said something more powerful and meaningful but a great way to put a scary cat like me in my place. She said, "I understood." She said she saw that I wasn't familiar with help. She went on to coach me on how to let her help me. She is a trained, experienced professional, and everything will be okay.

Katrina had worked for me before when she was a teenager, and I was managing retail. I had trained her in customer service, but over the years, she had become even more proficient in refining her skills, mastering the details, and handling things with a level of excellence that I should have recognized without question. Yet,

I found myself resisting, not because she wasn't capable, but because I was battling something deeper within myself.

Fighting against her was like fighting my reflection. How could I not trust her when I had trained her? How could I doubt her abilities when I could see her doing exactly what needed to be done? And yet, I struggled. That struggle wasn't about Katrina. It was about me.

It all came down to fear. Fear of losing control. I had asked for help, and I got it. I had prayed for help, and it showed up. And now, standing in front of me, was the very person I had once poured into, now fully equipped and capable, offering me the help I had longed for. But instead of embracing it, I was afraid of losing the help I had wished for, surrendering control, and what it meant to let go and trust truly.

The Balance of Power and Trust

This struggle of asking for help, receiving it, and then fearing the very thing we longed for also happens in intimate relationships. In any healthy relationship, there is always an element of power and control. The key difference between a healthy and toxic dynamic is that power and control are given freely in a healthy relationship. It's a natural give-and-take, much like a seesaw. One person shows, the other receives, and the motion continues. No one feels threatened, manipulated, or left powerless. The balance remains intact as both partners trust each other to maintain it.

Yet, surrendering control and genuinely letting go are often where we get stuck. A gospel song says to pray, surrender, and shift. I've done the praying. I've told God I surrender. I've promised I will do "Whatever You ask me to do. Wherever You send me, I will go." I poured all my energy into carrying out the vision I believed God placed in my heart to help women globally and bring harmony to the masses. And yet, in my mind, I kept doubting myself. I kept questioning the help I had asked for. I kept saying I just wanted to help others, never stopping to think about how this journey would impact me, my personal growth, and my relationships. It has. It did.

One of the most defining moments of this journey was planning a mission trip to Uganda with Katrina. We are now going international. We spent nearly two years preparing; for me, it was completely uncharted territory. I had never been on an overseas mission trip. We are going to the other side of the planet. We were headed to Uganda. The idea of empowering women and helping them build better lives fueled me. I am in my element of assisting people to be a better version of themselves. The plan was a two-day conference with 100 women from different faiths, hosted with the help of a local pastor. While fewer women attended than we had initially expected, the event was a success. It sparked something greater for women, spreading the word and lifting each other. Katrina and I had done something on an international stage. Something that would forever impact both of us.

Then, in January 2025, Sisters Arise was born. The 40 women from that first conference have grown into a movement of over 200 women from various faiths, all eager to be part of something bigger. What was intended to be 100 women has now doubled. Behind the scenes, business, personal, and ministry-related decisions had to be made. Each choice carried weight, requiring discernment, wisdom, and a deep understanding of the culture we were working within. There is no more thinking in English, Western values, or American traditions. If I do some of the same things now that I did with Katrina, it sends a ripple effect in languages of English, Swahili, Luganda, and several others. How would these people read my fear versus Katrina? How do I know Katrina's fears at this stage? My God, I have to get myself together.

So, how do you positively influence women from a different culture with limited resources in a country that isn't yours? Let me assure you that you can't show resistance, disorganization, or fear.

The answer is the same as in any relationship: trust the process, respect the balance, and surrender control when needed. We cannot empower others while clinging to fear and doubt. We cannot lead without trusting those ready to walk alongside us. We must be willing to shift from insecurity to confidence, from hesitation to action, from control to faith. Only then can we truly create change.

What It Means to Be at the Crossroads

At this moment, I realize that a crossroad is the same two paths that cross each other. Pain and love can cross. Navigating self-sacrifice in relationships is a delicate dance between giving and receiving. Being at a crossroads is more than just facing a difficult decision; it's a defining moment that forces you to evaluate where you are and where you want to go. It's not always a good place, and it's not necessarily a bad place. It's just where you are at this time. Sometimes, you are where you are supposed to be; sometimes, you are not. It's the space between where you've been and where you're headed, often filled with uncertainty, fear, and the weight of responsibility. You may be torn between staying in familiar territory or stepping into the unknown at these moments. The choice isn't always easy and doesn't have to be. The resources or support available will impact your ability to move forward. You are being told this, so don't be shocked when it happens or how it happens.

It's going to happen.

When you have the necessary resources, emotional support, financial stability, or a clear sense of direction, the crossroads may feel like an exciting opportunity for growth. You can confidently weigh your options, seek guidance from trusted sources, and take calculated risks. Decisions made from a place of security often lead to progress and fulfillment. You can embrace change with resilience, knowing you have the tools to navigate whatever comes next. You have to do it.

Standing at the crossroads can feel overwhelming when you lack resources, whether it's financial means, emotional support, or clarity. Fear of failure, self-doubt, and external pressures can cloud judgment, making it tempting to remain stagnant or choose the most straightforward path rather than the right one. Without support, you may feel you're making decisions in isolation, second-guessing every step. In these moments, it's crucial to focus on what you do, your inner strength, past experiences, and your ability to seek out new opportunities. Sometimes, moving forward requires asking for help, shifting your perspective, or taking small steps rather than giant leaps. It is worse to seek help from those that's incapable of assisting, especially when they are taking advantage of you and your resources.

No matter the circumstances, being at a crossroads is an opportunity for growth. Pain and love often meet at the crossroads, where choices carve the path forward. One can't exist without the shadow of the other; love deepens, pain lingers, and in between, we decide whether to let one define the journey or embrace both. You can embrace both.

Turing Right, Left, Keeping Straight, or Turing Back at a Crossroads, Acknowledge Where You Are

The first step in moving forward is recognizing that you are at a crossroads. Getting stuck in indecision is easy, but clarity begins with honesty. Ask yourself: What has brought me to this moment? What fears or uncertainties are holding me back? Acknowledging your reality gives you the power to assess your options without denial or avoidance. Not knowing which direction to go begins to clear once you recognize that you all know how to do it.

Define What You Truly Want

When faced with a difficult decision, separating expectations from your desires, cutting off deadbeats from sucking on your emotional resources, or giving yourself time to heal. This means choosing yourself and prioritizing your well-being over obligations, toxic attachments, and unrealistic expectations. Each is a process—a worthy one.

Weigh Your Options Without Fear

Fear often clouds your ability to see possibilities. Instead of focusing on what could go wrong, consider what could go right. You can plan for the worst, identify some risks, and build for the rewards. You can do it this way. You can.

Examples of Weighing Your Options Without Fear:

1. **Career Change Decision**: You've been in the same job for years but feel unfulfilled and dream of starting your own business. Fear tells you, "What if I fail?" What if I lose my financial stability? Instead of focusing on the risks alone, consider the possibilities: What if my business succeeds? What if I gain more freedom and fulfillment? Weigh the options: stay in your job with security but no growth, or take the risk and start small, building your business while keeping your job. Advice from a successful entrepreneur could help you navigate the transition with less fear.

2. **Leaving a Toxic Relationship**: You've been in a relationship that drains you emotionally, but you fear leaving because What if you end up alone? What if I regret my decision? Instead of dwelling on those fears, ask yourself: What if I find peace? What if I discover self-love and healthier relationships? Listing out your options, staying and enduring emotional pain, or leaving and creating space for healing can help you see the bigger picture. Talking to a professional or trusted friend can provide perspective, but ultimately, the choice is yours.

Seek wisdom from trusted mentors, but remember that the decision ultimately belongs to you. Growth requires risk;

sometimes, the only way to know if a path is correct is to take the first step. Family, friends, and others can be toxic.

Let Go of Control and Embrace Trust

Not every answer will come immediately, and not every outcome will be predictable. Surrendering control doesn't mean giving up; it means trusting that the right opportunities will unfold as you intentionally move forward. It's good because you start to make the right choices. Sometimes, we resist because we fear losing what we have, we fear losing the ground we have gained, but holding on too tightly in reality keep us from receiving something greater. The same hands gripping old problems can't be open to receiving new solutions. Clinging to old issues, past mistakes, or limiting beliefs hinders your ability to embrace new opportunities and solutions. Just as hands tightly gripping something cannot receive anything new, a mind preoccupied with past struggles cannot see or hold on to fresh perspectives. Growth requires letting go of what no longer serves you, allowing you to make space for better possibilities.

Take Action, Even If It's Small

Once you've considered your options, commit to action. The worst decision is no decision at all. Even if unsure, take one small step in the right direction. Momentum builds confidence, and clarity often comes after we move. Be willing to adjust along the way, but don't let uncertainty keep you stagnant. Adjust as many times as you need to.

There is no correct number of adjustments.

Trust That the Path Will Unfold

Every crossroads is an invitation to grow. The unknown may feel intimidating, but you have faced uncertainty and found your way through resilience, reflection, and action. Moving forward isn't about perfection; it's about progress, learning from what you have already done, from those past experiences, and embracing change, even when it feels uncomfortable and unfamiliar. Growth happens when you let yourself take on fear, take small steps, and trust yourself. The journey will not always be straightforward, but staying stuck in the familiar out of fear only limits your potential. Every step forward, no matter how small, brings you closer to something greater.

Not Your Problems

You'll meet people stuck, searching, or passing through at every crossroads. Some will have strong opinions about what you should do. Others will unload their fears, doubts, and distractions onto you. It's easy to absorb their theories, take on their problems, or get caught up in their chaos. But remember, their crossroads is not yours. Listen, support, and learn, but don't carry what isn't meant for you. Your path is yours to walk, and clarity comes when you focus on your direction, not the noise around you.

Never Turn Back Once You Reached the Crossroads

Reaching a crossroads in life symbolizes a crucial moment of decision. When you find yourself at this juncture, it's important to remember that you left your previous situation for a reason.

1. **Progress Requires Moving Forward**: Life is about growth; every decision shapes your path. Going back means stagnation, and the same old pain, while moving forward opens doors to new possibilities.

2. **Lessons Come from the Unknown**: The road ahead, though uncertain, holds the potential for experiences that will teach and strengthen you in ways you can't yet imagine.

3. **Regret is a Heavy Burden**: Turning back may leave you with lingering questions of "what if?" instead of allowing you to embrace the adventure in the unknown.

4. **Challenges Build Character**: Every choice comes with obstacles, but overcoming these challenges makes you wiser and more substantial.

5. **Comfort Zones are Traps**: While the familiar may feel safe, true success and fulfillment lie in your ability to embrace change and venture into the unfamiliar.

Chapter 4: Crossing Over The Crossroads

Sometimes, we encounter moments that symbolize transcendence, commitment, and a fearless acceptance of our destiny. Crossroads present us with choices—some familiar and others uncertain—but making a decision means more than simply choosing. It involves stepping into a new phase, drawing on past lessons, current realities, and future aspirations. Clarity arises not from hesitation but from understanding what we genuinely want rather than what is expected. We can transform a choice into a significant transition by letting go of burdens and trusting our journey, reassured by the wisdom of our past experiences.

So, here I am, my voice unheard, my hand steady but with a tingle of hesitation. I am standing at the crossroads to cross. I know I am still anticipating the pain, and deep down, it's not love.

There are moments in life when we stand at a crossroads, fully aware that our decision is incorrect. Yet, we can't always explain fear, pressure, comfort, or even exhaustion. We step forward anyway. It is a must. We tell ourselves we'll make it work, that things will change, that we'll figure it out along the way. If you are fortunate, you can find someone to blame temporarily. And if you are even luckier, they will accept the blame even if it's not their fault. It doesn't fix your problem. It just kicks the can down the road for a little while. Your only goal is to feel good, if only for a moment.

Deep down, though, we already know the truth: this path will lead to regret and struggle, and as usual, there will be a lesson we weren't ready to learn.

The Sensation to Bust a Move

You have that sensation to "bust a move." The phrase "bust a move," which originated in the 1980s, means to start dancing or taking action, especially boldly or energetically. It became popular through hip-hop culture and is often used to encourage someone to dance or take initiative. This is how you can feel when you are standing at a crossroads.

Crossing over the crossroads in this way is not always an act of recklessness. Sometimes, it's a reflection of where we are emotionally. We may not be strong enough to resist, or we may be tired of standing still. Here, we go back to doing something better than doing nothing. The unknown can feel unbearable, and even a wrong decision can seem better than making no decision. We convince ourselves that movement is still progress, even in the wrong direction.

But what happens when we cross that line when you bust a move? When we take that step, we know we shouldn't. Reality begins to settle in, and so does the weight of our choice. That feeling of a mistake, knowing it's a mistake at the beginning of the error, most of the time long before you continue to make it. We have turned warnings into acceptable consequences. We no longer ask ourselves, 'Why didn't I listen?'

Knowing I would make a mistake didn't require someone more experienced to point it out—I had the experience myself, yet I still didn't listen. It's a humbling reminder of how often we betray our wisdom. We make choices we recognize aren't in our best interest but convince ourselves otherwise. It's not that foolishness is more potent than wisdom; instead, the struggle between the two matters. In the moment of decision, our wisdom often takes a backseat to our desires, fears, and insecurities, leading us to make choices that we later regret. And in that internal conflict, real learning takes place. In these moments of conflict, we genuinely understand the power of our choices and the importance of listening to our wisdom, even when it's complicated.

Yet, even when making the wrong choice, something must be gained. I'm tired of saying it, and I know you're tired of reading it. But it's true. Every misstep carries a lesson. Every detour builds resilience. And sometimes, the very decision we knew we shouldn't make is the one that ultimately forces us to grow. Crossing over the crossroads isn't always about getting it right. It's about understanding why we didn't. When the lesson came full circle, we had another opportunity to stand at a crossroads again, only this time, with the wisdom to choose better. Learning from our mistakes and reflecting on our decisions gives us hope for the future.

My words hung in the air, heavy yet hopeful. It sounds like a simple question, I continued, more to myself than anyone else. My first thought is always to say, "Accept the love. This is the moment you've been waiting to receive it." I feel warm and fuzzy just thinking about it for a brief moment. But then, just as quickly, that feeling gets shoved aside by memories of all the sacrificial relationships I once called love. They were relationships where I constantly put the needs of others before my own, hoping that my sacrifices would be reciprocated. But they weren't. They were a mess, a hot mess. In these relationships, I lost myself in trying to please others and felt like I was constantly walking on eggshells, afraid to upset the delicate balance.

A" hot mess" is a situation, person, or thing that is chaotic, disorganized, or out of control—often amusingly or dramatically. "Hot mess" describes anything from a disastrous event to an individual whose life, despite being messy, is still somehow functioning. It is frequently used humorously or affectionately, acknowledging the disorder while recognizing some charm or resilience. Like I said, "a hot mess." I paused, allowing the weight of those memories to settle, each carrying its burden. The gravity of past decisions is something we all have, a reminder of the importance of our choices. It's okay to feel the weight of these decisions. It's a sign that we're aware of their impact and that awareness is the first step towards making better choices in the future.

My first instinct is to pray. I've been doing that for as long as I can remember. It's like a reflex. Whenever I know I have to do something different, I pray. I glanced down at my hands, and even as I started writing these thoughts, I stopped and prayed. Then something hit me. Prayer has become my weapon of stagnation. It's not that prayer is the issue, but rather how I've used it. I've used it as a crutch to avoid making difficult decisions or taking responsibility for my actions. Instead of using prayer as a source of strength and guidance, I've used it to escape my problems. Prayer has been weaponized against my judgment, abilities, capabilities, experiences, and wisdom. Not God, prayer. This realization has made me more introspective about my decision-making process, and it's a struggle I continue to grapple with.

The room goes uncomfortably quiet. As the words sank in, I remained unexpectedly sharp.

Don't get me wrong. Meaningful prayer is a beautiful thing. If it brings you comfort like it does me, I know why I do it, and you likely do it for the same reason. It makes me feel like I belong. I'm building a deeper spiritual understanding. But it also makes me self-sabotage. I become my sacrifice. This feeling goes beyond humility and stupidity. And that's where I get stuck. This is where things become a void. This is when my senses become numb. Changing it? Do I change it now? How can I change it now? My goodness, I have to change it now.

There was a soft exhale as if it was releasing years of realizations.

These insights didn't come to me overnight. They result from years of walking with the pain and countless conversations with couples, families, single women and men, elders, divorcees, young people, givers, receivers, and takers about relationships. The successes and failures of those I've spoken to have become a blur, all blending. But one pattern stands out. When women first start dating, they often choose 'projects'-partners that make them feel needed. And I was no different. I always went for the neediest ones. The worse he was, the better I felt. I am not talking about the one wearing basketball socks with church shoes. I am talking about how he wore church shoes to play basketball when he was supposed to attend church.

My tone shifted, lighter, almost wry. I recognized this pattern but didn't want to break it.

My first date? He needed a date.

My first prom? The guy's original date backed out three days before.

My first marriage, at age 23? (As I let out a dry chuckle.) He needed a place to live. I had a job and good credit, so we married to keep him off the streets. Yes, I went all the way. I went past stupidity. And I did it with a straight face.

Are you seeing my patterns? Are you able to see yours? We are a hot mess.

My smile faded, and my voice dropped to a whisper. That marriage was my introduction to domestic violence.

I looked up, my eyes glaring into nothing. And it wasn't love or like—not even close.

We were married in a church. Before family, before friends, and most importantly, before God. It was a quick wedding, but my gosh, it was beautiful. My friends and family made sure of that. They pitched in to make it a lovely day to remember. But let me be honest: days, months, and years before the ceremony, I knew it was a mistake. I knew I was going to make a mistake like this. I don't know why I couldn't prevent it. I had counseled so many others. And I did it, too.

You might ask, 'Why didn't anyone say something?' Trust me, I asked myself this over and over. Truth is, I didn't need them to say anything. I was going to make this mistake regardless. But here's what I told myself: My family and friends worked hard. The invitations have already gone out. The gifts are sitting there, wrapped and ready. I can't stop now. It's too late. I never realized that making a mistake is never too late. You don't turn down the wrong direction on the highway and keep going. You stop and turn around because if you keep going, you bring other people to catastrophe.

I remember standing at the church door, my heart pounding not with excitement but with dread. Runners have this analogy when they're on the track, and they run at top speed for so long or for a long distance and enter into that last curve, the final stretch. Your legs are so tired of turning that curve that it feels like an 800-pound gorilla has jumped on your back. I knew I was about to stand before God and everyone I loved and tell the biggest lie of my life: a lie, y'all. It's a lie as big as that gorilla.

I looked at myself in the mirror, and you know what I saw? A beautiful bride. My mother had crafted my hairpiece with her own hands. Each silk rose and pearl was placed with so much love. The flower arrangements were a gift from my mother's friend, who owned a shop. My sisters and mother hand-sewed the dresses. Every detail of that day was a labor of love.

So, I told myself, "You can't back out now. They'll be hurt. Your family and friends will be hurt. You owe them this. This is for them as much as it is for me and my husband." Pleasing my emotions and using my family as the reason to bust this move was more potent than lying to myself, them, and God. A lie isn't always spoken words or misleading the truth. A lie is anything that is not accurate, authentic, or affirmation.

I took a deep breath, curved my lips into a small, practiced smile, and turned to face my future. I turned right into a lie.

This lie would not only haunt me emotionally but lead to me being abused.

And here's the part that haunts me: I discovered I wasn't alone in my doubt years later. They knew. My family and my friends knew that the wedding shouldn't have happened. We all participated in that mistake, but it's not anything I blame them for. I was the conductor of that train—the Orchestra and the roller coaster. And if I had just spoken up, they would've understood. They would've supported me. It would have been a much more valuable lesson. You don't have to make a mistake when you know it's a mistake.

But I didn't. I chose to be an intentional sacrificial lamb. I convinced myself that sparing their feelings mattered more than my happiness. And because of that decision, I spent the next year drowning in pain. It was never a day without anticipating pain; I woke up each morning and went to sleep, knowing I was going to wake up to pain.

You see, that's the thing about domestic violence. When you read the stats like the CDC saying that 1 in 4 women and 1 in 6 men will experience abuse in their lifetime, but when it's you, you don't think about statistics. You don't think you're one of them.

Back then, I didn't even know what domestic violence was. All I knew was what I'd been told: Be a good wife. Make your husband happy. That's one of your jobs. And so, I tried. Nobody ever says that a bad husband can be a good person or a good person can be a lousy wife.

But once the physical abuse started, my family stepped in. That's all I needed to find my way out. I wish I'd realized that I never needed to be abused to know I didn't need abuse.

The physical violence ended with the distance, but the emotional wounds? Those lingered.

I traded one type of abuse for another. I threw myself into work, filling my days to keep the pain at bay. It worked until the day ended, and the quiet came. That's when I slip on the mask. You know the mask I'm talking about, the one they called the strong Black woman. Back then, it was the era when Women were doing it for themselves. See how I capitalized the "w" in women it's not supposed to be. The commercials told us we could earn the money, be independent, care for the house, and still keep him happy. We all traded one abuser for another one. Corporations, governments, and every other peddler are selling us hope through loneliness—a single human abuser for a corporate and government abuser. Neither the corporations nor governments fixed anything. Nothing! Like billions of others, I bought into it. It was easier to wear the mask than the others wearing the same mask. But every time I sat alone and got quiet, the reality crept in. What I want! What I wanted was to love and be loved.

Moving with Intention, Not Just Motion

Let's be honest; we've all stood at a crossroads, knowing that the choice ahead of us wasn't right. And yet, we moved forward anyway. Maybe we told ourselves we could make it work, that things would change, that something good would come from it. But movement for the sake of movement is not progress. Sometimes, it's just movement without meaningfulness.

It's time to stop being the conductor of our destruction, leading ourselves into situations we already know will bring pain. You don't just bust a move to be doing it.

1. **Acknowledge the Pattern**: I recognize when I'm making choices out of fear, habit, or wishful thinking instead of truly aligning with my values, well-being, and wisdom. I've caught myself in cycles before and now I pay closer attention to how they start. This includes my mentality and physical behavior.

2. **Pause and Reflect**: Before moving forward, I ask myself: Is this right for me, or am I just trying to convince myself that it is? Leave it for a while. If it's still on my mind I self-reflect, saves me from unnecessary pain.

3. **Own My Choices**: I take responsibility for my decisions, whether they lead to success or struggle. Growth happens when I stop blaming circumstances or others and fully own my actions. I remember that lies are not always done with words. Lies don't always need a story.

4. **Move with Intention**: I remind myself that not all movement is progress. If I'm moving forward, it needs to be purposeful and

aligned with my goals, not just a way to stay busy or avoid discomfort. Taking to time to reset, refresh, and strategize is equally important.

5. **Set Boundaries and Standards**: I protect my future by making choices that truly serve me, so I can reciprocate fairly, not just those that feel familiar or easy. I've realized that walking away from what I know is wrong is as powerful as stepping toward what is right.

This mindset shift has made a massive difference for me. I realized I've done it the other way for so long that what is currently correct always feels wrong. I'll get over that at some point. Have you ever found yourself in a similar cycle?

Take Ownership

To take ownership is not only admitting you need something or someone. You must take ownership of the situation, your actions, the lies, and the way forward. Instead, we must take ownership of our choices and well-being, not for others' comfort. This means that taking ownership isn't just about admitting you need help or acknowledging a situation; it's about fully accepting responsibility for your actions, decisions, and the truth, even when it's uncomfortable. Actual ownership means being accountable for your path forward rather than shifting responsibility onto others or making choices to please them. Instead of prioritizing others and comfort, you must take responsibility for your well-being and choices. Your choices!
Our past experiences shape our decisions, whether a failed relationship or a career setback. They should not be overlooked;

they form the foundation for our future choices. Imagine standing at a literal crossroads, needing to choose one of several paths.

In life, we often find ourselves at a similar juncture where we must make decisions that will significantly impact our future. Life constantly presents us with moments where our choices shape our path forward—whether big or small, these decisions can influence our careers, relationships, and personal growth. The key is to approach them with awareness, responsibility, and a willingness to own the outcomes, good or bad.

Have you been facing a vital decision recently? How do you plan to bust a move?

You will realize that every choice isn't right, yet you need to proceed anyway—not solely out of fear, comfort, or exhaustion, but also from the courage that drives you forward. We rationalize our decisions, hoping for the best outcome. When our ignored warnings come to fruition, we ask, "Why didn't I listen?" This moment is a humbling reminder of how often we betray our wisdom. Are that voice from the past of parents or wise people saying, "I told you so, I tried to tell you, or a hardhead gets a sore butt?" Even incorrect choices can provide valuable lessons. Each misstep contributes to our growth, and every detour helps us build resilience. The key is to learn from these past experiences so that next time, we can make better choices.

Faith Without Action Keeps You Stuck

I've prayed and asked for guidance. But if I'm honest, sometimes I've used prayer to delay action, to avoid making the tough decisions I already knew I needed to make. Prayer is powerful but never meant to replace movement or self-motivation. Stop hiding behind worship.

Faith Requires Action

The next step is trusting that I already have the wisdom, strength, and experience to make better choices. I refuse to stay in cycles of self-sacrifice, waiting until I'm drowning to seek help. Instead, I choose to move intentionally forward with purpose. It does require more than that.

Choosing Love Without Losing Myself

Love is not a sacrifice. My worth is not measured by how much I endure. I don't have to stay on a painful path just because I started it. If I know I'm making a mistake, I have the power to correct it. Fear, guilt, and obligation will no longer keep me in places that no longer serve me. Moving forward means embracing the love I deserve, mutual, nurturing, and genuine emotions—no more projects. Wear whatever socks you want. No more proving my worth through pain. Just love, freely given and freely received.

The Trap of Constant Busyness

Being busy didn't give me time to realize I didn't have to make the mistake of marrying someone I was never supposed to marry. There's a dangerous belief that we're making progress if we're always busy. If we keep moving, working, and filling every moment with activity, we won't have to deal with what's happening beneath the surface. But constant busyness is not the same as productivity; it's another way to avoid reflection, strategizing, and planning. When there's nothing to do, that's not a void to fill; it's an opportunity. A pause doesn't mean failure; it means space to think, evaluate, and plan. What have I done? What worked? What didn't? What needs to change? If I never stop to ask these questions, I'll keep running in circles, mistaking movement for progress. Athletes will tell you that practicing doesn't have the same effects as game-speed practice. Instead of fearing stillness, I need to embrace it. Let it be a moment of clarity and refreshing myself rather than useless movements. The real work isn't just in what I do; it's in understanding why I do it and making sure I'm headed in the right direction.

Seek Wisdom Before Making Life-Altering Decisions

Is it better to look stupid than be stupid? When faced with life-changing decisions, emotions often cloud judgment. Fear, desperation, or even excitement can push us into choices we haven't considered. But if you have access to someone with wisdom who has been where you are, who has made mistakes and learned from them, you owe it to yourself to seek their guidance before you act. A wise person won't decide for you, but they will challenge you to think beyond the moment. They will ask the hard questions, the ones you might be avoiding. They will remind you that a temporary feeling should not dictate a permanent choice. If you have someone like this, don't wait until after the mistake is made to seek their counsel. A conversation today could save you years of regret.

Chapter 5: The Giver's Dilemma

It's a silent battle, pouring your all into others while feeling empty, believing love is earned through sacrifice, yet feeling unseen when no one pours back. How can you teach others to value you if you never value yourself enough to receive? In everything I did, I showed you that by this kind of hard work, we must help the weak, remembering the words the Lord Yeshua himself said: It is more blessed to give than to receive (Acts 20:35). Umm! Regardless of your religious beliefs, this quote speaks to the universal struggle of over-giving.

You may have read thus far and felt uneasy upon encountering a biblical quote or scripture, especially if it doesn't align with your beliefs. If you continue with me, you'll understand why I include scriptures and quotes from various sources throughout this book. They have shaped who I am. But they have also, at times, held me back during specific periods of growth. When applied correctly, the proper knowledge is a tool for development, but when misused, it becomes a burden. There is a fine line between wisdom that frees you and beliefs that confine you. So, please stick with me; I promise I am not here to preach.

I was the one who gave, gave, and gave in relationships, including everything from love to money. I was the one who did most of the compromising and sacrificing. It was me who did the bending and shifting to make things work. I often got the worst of it. What's strange is that those scriptures did offer some aid.

Too often, I was the 'rock' when I should have been the 'hammer.' I was the one providing stability and support when I should have been the one initiating change and setting boundaries. I was the quiet one when I should have been voiceful. I was the problem solver when I should have let people figure it out for themselves. I was the nurturer when I should have been the one kicking some...

Setting firm boundaries is a crucial aspect of healthy relationships that we often overlook. But it's never too late to learn and implement this critical skill.

And in return? Silence. Neglect. Abused. At best, it was a vague acknowledgment of my efforts or a hint of something worthy, but never the reciprocity I longed for. I never knew what I needed to make myself a whole person, an appreciated woman, a recognized being. Somewhere along the way, I convinced myself that love was about giving, not receiving. Giving and not receiving were often confirmed by others. They would remind me frequently. Too often. That my strength was measured by how much I could endure, what pains I could take, and who dished it onto me didn't matter. They say it's better to give than receive. 'They say!' 'They say it a lot!'

The Quiet Moments

Deep down, I always knew something was missing. If all those giving things are true, why did I feel empty after I endured it? I felt it in the quiet moments when no one was around to need me. I knew this wasn't the whole truth, that real love wasn't supposed to feel like a one-sided obligation. Yet, I ignored that feeling. Worse, I ignored common sense. But in those quiet moments, I found the power of self-reflection, a tool that can guide us toward a more fulfilling life.

In those quiet moments, it was like a calm ache, a subtle but persistent void that no effort or giving could seem to fill. And I had tried. I had given all of myself, piece by piece, until I wasn't sure what was left. If everything people said about love were true, requiring patience, selflessness, and sacrifice, why did I feel so hollow after enduring it? Why the emptiness? Why did I give so much of myself that I didn't recognize myself? I did not recognize myself!

It wasn't the grand moments that revealed the truth to me. It wasn't the arguments, the disappointments, or the exhaustion that made me question everything. It was the silence. The quiet moments when no one was around to need me. Strangely, I knew the people were misusing my attention, presence, and love, but I still wanted it. I wanted that pain so bad that I would volunteer myself for it. By this time, I become conditioned. When I wasn't being helpful or offering, fixing, or holding someone else together, that's when the emptiness spoke the loudest. These were the moments when I was left alone with my thoughts, and the realization of my own needs and desires became painfully clear. That's the quietest noise you will ever hear.

I had spent so much time believing love was about giving that I forgot to ask whether it was ever meant to be received, too. I had absorbed the unspoken rule that to be worthy of love, I had to prove my value through sacrifice. This felt like a form of suffrage, a term often used to describe women's or human rights struggles. I thought love was something earned, not something freely given. I never thought of asking, "If everyone is giving, who is receiving?"

Then, I had to learn specifics. Different people like their love and attention given in various ways at certain times, so not only do you have to provide this, but you have to know precisely how each person likes it. You have to see how each customer likes their coffee or tea. There are endless ways to prepare and drink tea and coffee. If you have too much of one ingredient, you can ruin the entire experience for the drinker. To know this is tiresome. It's exhausting.

For a long time, I ignored the weight of that truth, and worse, I ignored common sense. You know it's common sense when you hear that little voice saying, "You know better, but you're going to do it anyway, aren't you."

Common sense told me love shouldn't be a one-sided obligation. It shouldn't feel like standing in a downpour with an empty cup, hoping someone else will notice I'm thirsty and fill it. It shouldn't feel like apologizing for needing warmth when I had spent years setting myself on fire to keep others comfortable. After you think it is helpful to light the fire, you feel burnt up like a matchstick and weather away in the wind.

But I was good at rationalizing. Whenever I felt like I should be more selfish, the scriptures would put me back in my place. I told myself that love was hard work, and this was just the price of it. And here come other people to reintegrate, and you are supposed to give more than you receive—all the while they are receiving. I said to myself that the profound loneliness I felt was just a phase, something that would pass if I could be more patient, more understanding, whatever I hadn't yet become. A guy like Moses (in the Bible) had done it for 40 years. Few in the Bible suffered more than Job. He had a good family, a respected name, and great wealth. But Satan challenged Job's faith, arguing that his devotion was tied to his prosperity. With God's permission, Job lost everything: his wealth, his children, and even his health. His friends accused him, and his wife told him to curse God, yet Job refused. He grieved, he questioned, but he never let go of his faith. His story wasn't just one of suffering but of endurance, proof that faith isn't built on blessings alone. Like many others, this story was a constant reminder that love and faith often require sacrifice, but it's important to remember that these stories were written differently. No sitcoms highlighted fantasy, no social media to pretend, and now nearly everyone can read and interpret things in their way and their lessons interpreted in many ways. All this goes on in your face 24 hours daily, 365 days a year.

Still, when the world was quiet and the expectations faded when I had nothing left to pour out, I couldn't shake the truth that gnawed at me. Genuine, authentic love wasn't supposed to feel like this. I wasn't expecting it all day, every day, but I wasn't getting it at all. Zero! Zip! Zilch! Zed! Zot! And maybe I wasn't meant to stay in a place where I had to convince myself otherwise.

I justified my self-sacrifice by telling myself that I was strong. My strength was encouraged by others, especially those sitting in scripture. I was always convinced that others needed me. It creates stress and anxiety if I am disposable to them. I was never convinced I needed them, too. I could take the hit because I was tough enough to bounce back. They tell you God doesn't give you anything you can't handle. It's not supposed to feel comfortable. I became the go-to person for everyone: friends, family, and even people who had done me wrong. And just like a boxer in training, I thought I was conditioning myself to handle the blows. And just like a boxer, the reward is the main event to showcase those months of the harshest training, but in real life, in my life, your life, what is the main event? I didn't realize that there's no protective gear in real life. You can't put on gloves to soften the impact of emotional punches. And just like a fighter, those early hits don't always show their damage immediately. But over time, they accumulate. They settle in your body, on your mind, in your spirit, in the way you move through the world. Eventually, your body and mind will give out as designed. Boxers have a term for this, "punch-drunk," referring to boxers who, after taking too many blows to the head, became dazed, disoriented, or slow in their movements. Over time, it has come to describe anyone mentally or physically exhausted, confused, or dazed, whether from actual physical impact, extreme fatigue, or being overwhelmed. For example, I was so tired after pulling an all-nighter that I felt punch-drunk at work. He was punch-drunk from the endless stream of bad news and could barely think straight.

The Moment I Learned to Fight Back

Not every boxer has the same defensive strategy. Some fighters are willing to take a punch to land one of their own, trusting their toughness and power to outlast their opponent. Others rely on head movement, footwork, and precise timing, ducking, slipping, and dodging hits while waiting for the perfect counterpunch. Then, some prioritize complete avoidance, staying elusive and calculating, only unleashing a furious combination when they see an opening. Each approach has its strengths and weaknesses, but in the end, the best defense is the one that suits the fighter's skill set, mindset, training, preparedness, and strategy in the ring.

Like boxers have different defensive styles, people have various ways of handling life's challenges. Some are like fighters who take punches to give one back; they absorb everyone else's problems, always being there for others, even at their own expense and demise. They endure the emotional blows, believing their strength lies in helping, even if it wears them down. Others are more calculated, dodging their struggles by focusing on others and avoiding their pain while waiting for the right moment to take care of themselves, except that moment never seems to come. And then some never let themselves get hit, keeping up a strong front, unleashing their energy to support others but allowing themselves the same care. In the ring of life, constantly taking hits for others without defending yourself eventually leads to burnout. A boxer can't fight forever without guarding themselves, and neither can you. At some point, you have to ask, when will I start protecting my well-being like I protect everyone else's?

Fighting back is the most challenging thing you can do when you don't know what you're fighting for and who you're fighting against.

Some boxers, just like you, use being on the offensive as their best defense. Instead of waiting, dodging, or absorbing hits, they stay aggressive, constantly pushing forward, keeping their opponent too busy to strike back. It's a relentless strategy that requires stamina, resilience, and an almost unstoppable drive. But just like in life, constantly being on the attack can be exhausting. You spend so much energy taking care of others, staying ahead of problems, and making sure everyone else is okay that you never stop to defend yourself. Just like the boxer who does too much in the beginning, there's no power left in the punch to put the opponent away. The problem is that even the strongest fighters get tired. And if you never take a moment to guard yourself, rest, and recover, you'll eventually have nothing to give. Being there for others is admirable, but don't forget, you're in this fight too. Who's in your corner when you need it? Who's there to help you prepare for the next battle regardless if you win or get knocked out?

In the fourth grade, the girls on the bus started picking on me. They called me names, made fun of me, pushed the limits of bullying, and made up lies.

"You think you're better than us." They were trying to portray me as a Miss Goody two shoes. I stayed quiet. I would just read my books as they were my haven, comfort, refuge, and escape from the world around me. But their taunts didn't stop. They kept at it for days, their words gnawing at me like tiny, relentless bites. And then, one day, they convinced a third grader to pull my hair and hit me. She grabbed one of my long ponytails and smacked me in the head.

That was it.

I fought back. I tried to grab her short hair, but when that didn't work, I did the only thing left to do: I punched her square in the face. Hard!

Everyone was shocked. Not just because I fought back but because I fought and I won.

And yet, despite defending myself, I was punished. I was kicked off the bus for a week. The same as the girl who attacked me. The difference? My mother could take me to school. Her mother couldn't. She missed school.

I felt sorry for her, so much so that I asked my mother to drive her, too. She accepted, and for a week, we rode to school together. We never became close friends, but something shifted. I didn't just earn her respect; I earned the respect of the kids at school.

I learned a valuable lesson. You can win a fight and still lose; somehow, that loss can be the biggest win in life.

The Disguise of a Giver

As I said for days, they kept at it, their words gnawing at me like tiny, relentless bites. I succeeded at ignoring them to the point that they had to become physical.

As a giver, you must disguise your concerns because your only concern is others. As a giver, you learn early on that your concerns must be buried beneath reassurances, masked by a steady voice, softened into something palatable. Your worries are not for airing but for swallowing because your only concern is others.

You become fluent in the language of self-sacrifice, speaking it so naturally that even you begin to believe your needs don't exist. You learn to silence your exhaustion with a smile, package pain in neat, labeled, unimportant boxes, and turn every "I need" into a "Don't worry, I've got it."

And maybe, at first, it feels like love. You see how happy the other person is, and you never think about anything beyond happiness for something as simple as appreciation. After all, love is about giving. Love is about showing up, pouring out, and ensuring no one else goes without. But what happens when you've given so much that there's nothing left of you? You start with a box of love; one day, you reach inside the box for yourself, and it's empty.

No one notices the weight you carry when you make it look effortless. No one asks if you're okay when you're always the one asking first. And sometimes, you make sure you're the first one to ask. Sometimes, you volunteer too quickly. And so, you keep going, pouring, and showing up until you realize you're empty one day, and no one is there to back you up. The worst feeling is when surrounded by people incapable of doing it.

But a giver is not meant to be invisible. Love is not meant to be a one-way street. The most challenging lesson is this: you are allowed to need, too.

Our Stories Begin Long Before Adulthood

I share these childhood stories because who we are as adults didn't begin at eighteen. We don't just wake up one day and decide to be the person we are. We don't suddenly choose to be overly accommodating, an easy target, or someone who takes advantage of others. There's a pattern, a slow, steady shaping of our character based on the experiences we had growing up.

Think about it. The way you navigate relationships today, the way you react to conflict, the way you either stand up for yourself or shrink back, these aren't new habits. They've been forming for years.

So, take a moment to reflect. What youth experiences shaped how you love, fight, or surrender? Some memories may be joyful, others painful. However, how you respond still affects how you react now. And the best thing you can do for yourself is to stop, sit with those experiences, and learn from them. Because nothing, not time, not avoidance, not even sheer willpower, can take the place of a good moment of reflection.

The Weight of Giving Without Receiving

The weight of giving without receiving refers to the emotional, physical, or financial burden one might feel when they continuously give, whether it's love, support, resources, or effort, without receiving anything in return. When you give to relationships, work, or social situations, you are drained or unappreciated due to the intentional or unintentional reciprocation. It represents the strain and exhaustion that comes from imbalance. It evokes the image of carrying a heavy load that only gets heavier over time because there's no relief or replenishment. It symbolizes self-sacrifice, unreciprocated generosity, or the struggle of sustaining others while depleting oneself. Stop doing it!

Reclaiming Balance, Recognizing the Pattern

The first step in moving forward is recognizing the cycle of over-giving and under-receiving. Over-giving and under-receiving are two sides of the same coin, rooted in self-worth, boundaries, and relationship dynamics. The over-giver often enables the under-receiver, creating a reinforcing cycle. Breaking free requires setting boundaries, recognizing one's worth, and allowing a balanced energy exchange. Over-giving happens when someone gives excessively" time, energy, money, emotional support," often at their own expense. It stems from people-pleasing, a need for validation, or fear of rejection. You can also have been coerced or manipulated into doing it for years.

Under-receiving occurs when someone struggles to accept help, love, or resources, often due to low self-worth, guilt, or a belief that they must handle everything alone. You can also have been the giver for so long that you don't know how to receive.

It is easy to fall into the habit of self-sacrifice, especially when it has been ingrained since childhood. But acknowledgment, awareness, and admission are power. The moment you realize that you've conditioned yourself to prioritize others while neglecting yourself, you gain the ability to make a change. How rapidly you do depend on many factors, like how deeply ingrained the pattern is, your self-awareness versus falling back into the pattern, your willingness to set boundaries beyond the patterns, and the support systems around you. Healing isn't linear; it takes time and practice, and sometimes, there is discomfort. But when you recognize the imbalance, you take the first step toward change. Love and generosity should never come at the expense of your well-being emotionally, mentally, or physically.

Setting Boundaries without Guilt

One of the hardest lessons for a giver is learning to set boundaries. Boundaries are not walls; they are guidelines that define what you are willing to accept in your relationships. No one but you get to decide these boundaries. It is not selfish to say no, to ask for respect, or to demand reciprocity. You are not a bottomless well. You are not meaningless. You are not an empty vessel. You are not here to be drained. Start small. Add little boundaries here and there. Make small adjustments. When you say "no," explain less and less why you said no. If you always say yes immediately, practice pausing. Give yourself time to consider whether a request aligns with your own needs and well-being before responding. You can say, "Let me think about it first," to replace "yes," and then say no later. You can do it: one request, person, and situation at a time.

Understanding That Love is a Two-Way Street

Real love is not about proving your worth through suffering. It is not about enduring pain to demonstrate loyalty. The best romantic, familial, or platonic relationships are built on mutual effort, respect, and care. If you find yourself in a dynamic where you are the only one giving, ask yourself: Is this love or obligation? Love should feel like a shared experience, not a lonely endurance test. Not a one-way street.

Breaking Free from Conditioning

Conditioning, institutionalization, tradition, and culture can keep you stuck in patterns of doing what you have always done the way others expect, even at the expense of your well-being. These forces shape your beliefs about duty, sacrifice, and self-worth, making change feel impossible. But awareness is the key. Once you recognize these influences, you gain the power to question them, redefine your values, and reclaim your path.

Conditioning is the unconsciously learned behaviors, beliefs, and patterns through repeated experiences. It can come from family, society, or personal experiences.

Institutionalization is the reinforcement of norms, expectations, and behaviors by systems such as education, religion, government, or the workplace, making specific ways of thinking or acting feel obligatory.

Tradition: Practices and beliefs passed down through generations, often followed out of respect for history or cultural identity, sometimes without questioning their relevance.

Culture: The broader system of values, customs, and social norms that shape how people think, behave, and interact within a society or group. It influences identity, relationships, and life choices.

Social Conditioning: The process by which societal norms and expectations shape individual behavior, often leading people to conform without questioning whether those norms align with their values.

Obligation: A sense of duty or responsibility imposed by external expectations, often making individuals feel compelled to act in ways that may not align with their personal needs or desires.

Conformity: The act of adjusting one's beliefs or behaviors to align with societal, cultural, or group expectations, often at the expense of personal authenticity when it comes to spirituality or scripture to keep you in line with giving.

Doctrine: A set of beliefs or teachings upheld by a religious institution, often guiding moral choices and behaviors.

Dogma: Principles or beliefs considered unquestionable within a religious tradition, often shaping how followers interpret faith and life.

Obedience: The expectation to follow religious laws, leaders, or teachings without question, sometimes at the expense of personal discernment.

Ritual: Repeated religious practices or ceremonies that reinforce faith, tradition, and communal identity, sometimes followed without reflection on personal meaning.

Guilt: A feeling instilled by religious teachings when one deviates from prescribed beliefs or behaviors, often influencing decision-making and self-worth.

Salvation Anxiety: The fear of not meeting religious standards for spiritual redemption, which can lead to excessive self-sacrifice or rigid adherence to doctrine.

There are too many people-pleasing terms and phrases to list here. You probably know how you can become conditioned to behave one way by now.

Many of us were taught that strength is measured by how much we can carry. We were told that suffering builds character, and this is the truth. Being a good person means always putting others first. But this belief, when taken to an extreme, becomes a prison. It can become "social incarceration." It convinces us that our needs don't matter and that asking for something in return makes us weak, ungrateful, and selfish. That is not the truth. Strength is also knowing when to put the burden down. It is knowing when to walk away. Please watch this while you work through your process.

Refilling Your Cup

Refilling your cup means replenishing your energy, well-being, and emotional reserves before continuously giving to others. It emphasizes self-care, self-love, and setting boundaries to prevent burnout. If empty, you cannot pour your cup into others through support, love, or services.

It challenges the mindset that self-care is selfish and highlights that caring for yourself allows you to give from a place of abundance rather than depletion. This can involve rest, personal growth, receiving support, or simply allowing yourself to enjoy life without guilt.

1. Prioritize Your Own Needs First

- Permit yourself to rest without guilt.
- Ask yourself, "What do I need right now?" and honor the answer.
- Set boundaries with people who drain your energy.

2. Engage in Activities That Nourish You

- Spend time in nature, journal, or engage in creative hobbies.
- Move your body in a way that feels good, such as yoga, dance, or stretching.
- Listen to music, read a book, or watch something that makes you happy.

3. Receive Without Guilt

- Accept help, love, and kindness from others without feeling obligated to give back immediately.
- Practice saying "Thank you" instead of "You shouldn't have."
- Remind yourself that you are worthy of rest, love, and care like everyone else.

4. Take Care of Your Emotional & Mental Health

- Practice mindfulness, deep breathing, or meditation.

- Seek professional therapy or coaching, or talk to a trusted friend about your feelings. Do this regularly in the beginning until you know the habit has changed.
- Release guilt or limiting beliefs about self-worth and giving. Stop making "yes" your first response. Let's be honest: most people don't have enough critical things going on, so you always have to say yes.

5. Set Boundaries & Protect Your Energy

- Say "No" without over-explaining when something doesn't serve you.
- Reduce time with people who only take and never give back.
- Stop over-explaining or justifying why you need time for yourself.
- Stop being around lazy people.

6. Create Space for Joy & Play

- Laugh, have fun, and do things for pleasure, not productivity.
- Reconnect with things you loved as a child, like drawing, playing music, or daydreaming.
- Schedule moments of joy into your daily routine. It doesn't have to be significant. It just has to bring joy.

The key is consistency. Self-care isn't a one-time act; it's a lifestyle. Consider the areas you struggle the most with.

If you have spent your life giving to others, you may not even know how to give to yourself. Start by identifying what replenishes you. Is it solitude? Creativity? Moving around? Rest? Deep, meaningful conversations? Laughter? Acknowledgment?

Seek those things out intentionally. Make them a priority. You are just as deserving of care, love, and dignity as the people you pour into.

Choosing Reciprocity Over Relentless Giving

You don't have to stop being generous, friendly, or pleasant. You have to stop being a sucker. (Sucker: Someone who is easily deceived or taken advantage of "He's a sucker for a sob story." (Someone who is easily manipulated.) You don't have to become hardened, selfish, or surly. But you must be selective about who receives your energy and why.

Give to those who also give to you. Invest in people who see you, appreciate you, and try to meet you halfway. They might not have the emotional resources to do it, but at least they put forth a sincere effort you can recognize.

Accepting that Some Relationships Must End, so be Honest with the Truth

Not everyone will understand your shift. Especially the selfish people. Some will resent your newfound boundaries. Some will push back. Can you imagine that some people will be angry that you decided not to continue to be a sucker for their needs? Some relationships may not survive your growth, which should be perfectly okay. If a connection only thrives when you are overextending yourself, then it was never built on love or respect; it was built on your sacrifice. You deserve better.

Accepting that some relationships must end is never easy, but sometimes, it's necessary for your well-being and growth. Being honest with the truth means recognizing that you're the only one putting in the effort, while the other is just coasting or taking without giving back. It's accepting that no matter how much you try, love, or support them, they aren't meeting you halfway.

Instead of making excuses like "Maybe they'll change," "Maybe I'm expecting too much," "They've done more than others," or "At least they're still here," you face reality: a relationship isn't meant to be one person carrying all the weight. Once you accept that truth, you can choose: continue holding on to something that drains you or let go and make space for people who genuinely value and reciprocate your effort.

To be honest with the truth means fully accepting and acknowledging reality, even when it's uncomfortable or difficult. It's not just about telling the truth to others but also about being honest with yourself and facing facts without denial, excuses, or wishful thinking.

1. **Acknowledge the Truth**: Be honest with yourself about the relationship. Is it draining you more than it's fulfilling you? Are you holding on out of love, fear, or obligation? Recognizing when something is no longer serving you is the first step to letting go.

2. **Let Go of Guilt**: It's natural to feel guilty when stepping away from someone, but staying in a relationship that harms you emotionally, mentally, or even physically helps no one. Prioritizing yourself isn't selfish; it's necessary.

3. **Accept That Change is Part of Life**: Not every person is meant to stay forever. Some people come into your life to teach lessons, share moments, or support you for a season. They may be going through their issues at the time. When that season ends, it's okay to move on.

4. **Set Clear Boundaries**: If a relationship is toxic, one-sided, or no longer healthy, create boundaries that protect your peace. Whether that means reducing contact, having a final conversation, or cutting ties completely, do what's best for you.

5. **Feel Your Emotions Without Dwelling on Them**: Grieving the end of a relationship is normal. Allow yourself to feel sadness, anger, or relief, but don't let those emotions keep you stuck. Acknowledge them, process them, and then focus on healing.

6. **Redirect Your Energy to Yourself**: Instead of pouring your energy into a relationship that's no longer working, invest it in yourself. Focus on personal and professional growth, hobbies, new friendships, and self-care. The end of one relationship is often the beginning of something better.

7. **Trust That You're Making the Right Choice**: Doubt will creep in, especially if the person meant a lot to you. But trust that if a relationship needed to end, it was for a reason. Your future self will thank you for choosing peace, growth, and happiness over comfort and familiarity.

The Freedom in Letting Go

You will feel the weight lift when you stop giving to those who only take it. It won't happen all at once. Some of you can do it Immediately. In some cases, it is going to take years. You may even struggle with guilt, feeling bad, or feeling like you are betraying. The quiet moments will no longer feel hollow. They will feel complete—full of your presence, needs, and voice.

And that is where healing begins.

Your story is not one of loss. It is one of reclamation—reclaiming your energy, time, and worth. You are not here to be drained. You are here to live, love, and be loved in return. Stop making it more complicated than that.

1. **You will rediscover yourself.** When you stop pouring into those who only take, you'll have the space to reconnect with who you are beyond what you give to others. Your wants, dreams, and needs will no longer feel secondary; they will finally have room to exist.

2. **You will attract better connections.** As you reset your boundaries and prioritize yourself, the people who genuinely value and respect you will start to stand out. Relationships built on mutual care will replace those that once drained you.

3. **You will learn that peace isn't loneliness.** At first, the absence of constant giving might feel unfamiliar, even empty. But soon, you'll realize that peace isn't isolation; it's freedom to exist without exhaustion, give without depletion, and love without losing yourself.

Chapter 6: Trauma Grip

It's like the event keeps replaying, affecting emotions and actions, making everyday life overwhelming. A traumatic experience can take over someone's life, leading to feeling disconnected from themselves and the world around them, often causing them to withdraw from others and become emotionally numb. It's important to recognize these signs, as understanding them is the first step toward seeking help and finding ways to heal.

They say trauma keeps you in the past, and I've come to understand the truth in that. I feel like a giddy teenager when I'm with a man who loves me in ways I've never experienced. I blush, fumble, and doubt myself. This behavior seems incongruent with my age and experience. Instead of embracing love confidently, I recoil, expecting the pain I've grown accustomed to. This is the impact of trauma on personal relationships, a battle that many of us, including myself, face. The trauma I've endured has made it challenging to fully accept love, often leading me to anticipate pain and withdraw emotionally. This struggle is a constant reminder of the need for healing and self-empowerment in the face of trauma, and it's a battle I often find myself losing to self-sabotage. This self-sabotage, this constant struggle with the past, is a stark reminder of the need for understanding and empathy in the face of trauma. I share this not for pity but for understanding, to help you empathize with the daily struggle against the past that many of us face. It's a heavy burden, a weight that many of us carry, and you must grasp the profound influence of trauma on relationships and the urgent need for healing.

It was as if I was stuck in the mindset of my younger self, the one who first learned to fear rejection, loss, and heartbreak. No matter how much I grow, trauma whispers that love is dangerous and that happiness is fleeting. Trauma has a tight grip; it can be tighter than self-worth. This tight grip of trauma has made it difficult for me to form healthy and fulfilling relationships. It often leads me to anticipate pain and withdrawal emotionally, even when the relationship is going well. This struggle, this constant battle with the past, is a stark reminder of the need for healing and self-empowerment in the face of trauma. It's a heavy burden that I, like many others, carry. The impact of trauma on relationships is profound, shaping our perceptions and beliefs, and it's a burden that many of us carry, a burden that calls for sympathy and understanding to help you understand the daily struggles that many of us face. You must grasp the profound influence of trauma on relationships and the urgent need for healing.

As a young girl, I sought refuge in the captivating world of books. Being a sickly child, I was unable to engage in outdoor activities due to allergies. I didn't feel deprived; instead, I found solace in the pages of books, each a new adventure. Then, I made a significant discovery. I could immerse myself in romance novels. Oh, the things they put in books. These books, with their tales of love and adventure, inspired me and gave me hope. The trauma I experienced also influenced my relationship with books and reading. It shaped my understanding of love and relationships, often leading me to seek solace and inspiration in the pages of romance novels. The comfort and escape I found in these stories were a way to cope with the emotional turmoil caused by trauma, but they also influenced my perception of love and relationships, creating unrealistic expectations and a constant search for passion and adventure. While providing comfort, these novels also instilled in me a belief in love that is always effortless and perfectly timed, where soulmates magically understand each other without the need for honest communication or compromise. This experience underscores the profound influence of literature on our perceptions and beliefs and how it can shape our understanding of love and relationships. It's a testament to the power of storytelling in shaping our lives, and you must understand the power of literature in shaping perceptions.

This is just one example of how trauma can infiltrate various aspects of our lives, including our hobbies and interests, shaping our perceptions and beliefs.

A book can take you from a mental place of surprise or amusement. It can suggest amazement at the unexpected, bizarre, or shocking. You say I can't believe they wrote that! It can take you behind the criticism or skepticism. To imply doubt or disapproval of misleading, exaggerated, or controversial information. "Not everything in books is true, you know." In modern times, it reminds me of the internet and social media. A good book can go from admiration to nostalgia. It can reflect and capture appreciation for wisdom, beauty, or creativity. Books hold so much knowledge and wonder.

I found a passion for historical romance novels. I enjoyed them because they took me far off to lands, I could only dream of, and then they had the heroine fall in love and get married to her crush. I am a sucker for those books. Let me tell you about one of these novels that left a lasting impression on me. It was a story of love, adventure, and overcoming obstacles, shaping my understanding of what love should be like. This personal experience will help you connect with my journey, learning from the struggles I've faced and the hardship of moving forward.

I spent hours each day reading. I read until the early morning hours, then got up for school. I read while I ate, walked, and watched TV. I was never seen without a book. The library lady started looking for books because I was hard-pressed to find one, I hadn't read. By my teenage years, I was waiting at the bookstore for the next series of books to come out. I didn't have a personal romance I talked to my friends about, so I lived vicariously through my books. But oh, the joy of it all! The thrill of discovering a new world, the excitement of turning each page, the satisfaction of finishing a book and immediately reaching for the next one. Reading was not just a hobby but a passion, a lifeline, and a source of joy and comfort. It was my escape, my solace, my adventure. My relationship with books was deeply intertwined with my experiences of trauma and the coping mechanisms I developed. It was a way to navigate the complexities of love and relationships, and it continues to shape my perceptions and beliefs.

My romantic desires were shaped not only by the families in my neighborhood but also by the stories I read. I recall the families in my neighborhood. All but a couple of them were two-parent homes. Some of the mothers worked, but most of them stayed home and kept the house and children. I lived in a middle-class community where the families all knew each other. This also shaped how I feel the family should be. These experiences and the stories I read didn't just shape my desires and expectations in my home and community; they inspired a hopeful vision of love and family. The power of storytelling in shaping our desires and expectations is truly remarkable, and literature, in particular, played a profound role in shaping my understanding of love and relationships. It's a testament to the transformative power of literature in our lives. Reflecting on the role of literature in your own life and how it may have shaped your desires and expectations can be an enlightening experience. Literature can shape our understanding of love and relationships, and it's a journey worth exploring that can bring a new light to your understanding of love and relationships.

Back to romance and passion. Even with viewing families that worked together and were involved in their children's lives, I was hard-pressed to understand the passion around a relationship. I concluded that passion should be derived from books. One book in particular shaped what I constantly desired in a relationship. It has been quite a few years since I read the book, so I will not give the name. I will tell you what I remember about the storyline. This book's compelling storyline and personal experiences, which I'm about to share, profoundly influenced my understanding of passion and desire in a relationship. Let me take you back to a specific moment in my life that shaped my understanding of passion and desire in a relationship.

Let me tell you about a book that profoundly impacted my understanding of love and relationships. The heroine's name was Jenni. She was a young lady from France who had lost her mother at childbirth, and her father had remarried. Her father moved to the new colonies to make his fortune. He successfully built his empire around gold mining and was ready to bring his family to the new America. The book I will not name had a compelling storyline that deeply resonated with me. It shaped my expectations and desires, and to this day, it continues to influence how I view love and relationships. My personal experiences, such as the lack of romance in my life that I often discussed with my friends and how I lived vicariously through my reading, illustrate the profound influence of literature on our lives. These personal experiences help you connect with the narrative and understand the profound influence of literature on our lives.

Jenni, being his only child and raised to her teen years by her father, was allowed to learn things that were traditionally for men in the era. Jenni could ride a horse and shoot a gun and was well-educated. She was also proficient in the skills taught to gentle young ladies of the era, like sewing, needlepoint, playing an instrument, and flirting with young men. The way a young lady flirts with a suitor is an art form. In other words, Jenni was a well-rounded young lady. At the beginning of her character, Jenni fears moving to another country. She had heard rumors about savages and hardship. To be with her father excited her. But she had also felt she needed an adventure in her life.

Jenni found that once she made it to America, she would have to travel by land to the West because of the dangers of traveling to an undeveloped country. Jenni and her stepmother were given guards and a guide. The leading guide was Steve. Steve was what they called back then a half-breed. Steve was half Comanche. He had lived most of his life with the Comanche until he lost his wife and family to a raid. Steve was a rough man—a man of the land.

The perfect man for the job, Jenni's father thought. But what the father didn't bargain for was for Jenni and Steve to fall in love. Back then, no man wanted his proper young daughter to fall in love with a rough man. A non-adequate man. They desire their daughters to take a husband from a well-to-do family.

Jenni and Steve's relationship didn't start in love. They disagreed, and Steve rudely commented that Jenni was a delicate debutant. But that same passion for arguing led to the passion for love. He found out she was not as fragile as he thought. She found out he wasn't as mean as he pretended. One day, an argument ended in wild lovemaking. Decisions had to be made after that, and a relationship started. If you have ever read a romance novel, you know that it didn't go quite as smoothly as this. Plenty of ups and downs finally ended with them in marriage—a life happily ever after.

One time during their marriage, Steve had to leave and instructed Jenni not to leave the location until he returned. She would be safe if she stayed put. Jenni still didn't like taking orders, but she learned to trust Steve through the relationship. Supplies got low before he returned. She kept telling herself he loved her and would not leave her stranded. He knew the amount of supplies she had and would ensure she got more before she starved. The book takes the readers through the mental process Jenni went through as she fought with the fear that if she didn't leave and get what she needed, she would starve and never be found. But Jenni put her faith in what she knew of her husband. She stayed in place for about a week despite scarce supplies. She wanted to prove she had what was needed to be his wife in this underdeveloped, hostile, and harsh land.

After reading this series of books about their lives, I wanted that. I wanted to have a husband that I could trust with my life. I wanted a man to guide, show, and ensure me. I know that no matter what, he would do everything necessary to protect and provide for me. I wanted to trust so hard that I denied all the fear in my head that said, "I need to do it all myself." I wanted a relationship that was based on love that defied all odds. Searching for this love has made me vulnerable to personalities I feel we're in, Steve. Yes, I know that Steve is a fictional character. Yes, I know their adventures came from a woman's imagination. But my heart says it is possible. I have met these men in real life. I know they exist. I need one for myself. The Bible says God will give you the desires of your heart. My heart wants love that surpasses all understanding, rooted in trust and truth. Together, we can conquer the world. At least our world. At least a household. I have never given up on this dream. The problem is that the abuse, pain, and mistrust have left a protective veil around my heart.

Yes, Steve returned on time and brought supplies. I wonder if my Steve exists and if he will return in time. Is Mr. Opportunity my Steve or another man with survival traits I am attracted to? Women aren't attracted to bad boys who misuse them and break their hearts. Women want just a tad bit of adventure. Am I willing to move to a foreign land to find my happiness? You will have to read book two because the story is just beginning.

Because our relationship is long-distance, there are times when we don't talk much for a couple of days. I remember Jenni. I tell myself to believe that he is doing what needs to be done for family and business. But the trauma grip rears its nasty head. I started thinking of all the things he could be doing that were not right for me. All the women he may be doing it with. Then I become a weak woman and send nasty messages and voice mails. Messages he doesn't deserve. Messages about how he doesn't care about me. The entire time I am sending this message, I know it's not the right thing to do. This man is asleep. I don't know why I didn't send him a beautiful message. A message as though he is dreaming about me.

Self-sabotage has been a pattern in my relationships. If I ended, then I could justify my pain. I was the strong one. Then, everyone rallied around me to say how I needed to do it. Now I feel justified. I can justify how I tried; the other person didn't care. But then I end up sad, depressed, and lonely, back on the roller coaster.

I am determined not to pay the conductor to board again when this ride stops. There are so many other rides in the park that will bring joy. As you read this book, you will also decide when the next step in your healing process is that it is time to get off the roller coaster and stay off. At least that roller coaster that's causing you trauma. It's time to fight for the love that you want. It's time to trust again.

The little girl in me has protected me for many years. She has kept me from showing my true self and given me a way out of relationships. It is time to let her go. It is time for me to nurture the woman I have become. I have protected myself in many ways, primarily by keeping people at bay. If I am here, the other person has to be way, way, way over there. Not just intimate relationships but all relationships. I have friends, but only a few know who I am. They know who I am to them but not my personality. I don't let people in because I fear they will leave and not return. At least, that is what Trauma Grip says. It has a tight grip on me, y'all.

From this moment forward, I declare I will let my protective barrier down when needed. I will still use discernment and pray about situations; however, I will also listen. You see, the first person I must trust to be a good steward of my heart is myself. I stopped trusting myself and my decisions. I wanted to give my power away. Dr. Youngblood said something to me the other day that sent me into a tailspin. He said I had to decide if I wanted to be a leader. I had to decide if I wanted to lead my business or give my power over. This didn't sit well with me. I had let things spin so much in depending on the actions of others that I forgot to whom I say God gave this mission. I keep forgetting to listen to me. The me that knows.

Dr. Youngblood's statement hit me hard because God asked me the same question a few months ago. As I was praying and complaining to God one morning, the Holy Spirit spoke to me and said that I had been given my ministry as a leader and asked if I wanted it. I said yes and was told to get up and act like it. Fight for it. Strategize for it. Administer it. Operate it. At the time, I did, but I see I started moving back to giving up. Making the same excuses. Procrastinating in the same way. I want back to familiarity.

That trauma grip is firm.

I tell you this because there may be something you are trying to achieve and having a hard time moving forward. Please take a moment and do what I did. Write down what you started the project for. What outcome do you want to achieve? Then, determine who should be in charge. If that person is you, are you performing in your rightful position? If not, why? Don't try! Get it right!

My answer is that I have conditioned myself to play small so people around me are not offended or intimidated. I cannot do that and help the number of women I want to help. I have to be a leader. I am the solution for many. As the solution, I have to be visible and available. So do you. Get up. Take your rightful position.

Growing up, my brother would ask me questions and make me think. One day, he wondered what happens when an immovable object meets an irresistible force. For a long time, I tried to answer. I read the physics behind the question and how scholars have been attempting to answer it. I find myself asking the question again nowadays. Many say that domestic violence will always be with us. Families have been dealing with abuse since time began. This may be true for a long time, but I don't believe that is how we were created. I believe we were created as a family unit for healthy outcomes.

This is a well-known parable about making a difference, often called The Starfish Story. One morning, an old man walked along the beach after a big storm. The tide had receded, leaving thousands of starfish stranded on the sand. Without the ocean's waves to carry them back, they would soon dry out and perish under the rising sun.

As he walked, the old man saw a young boy up ahead, moving quickly and bending down often. Curious, he approached and saw the boy picking up starfish one by one and gently tossing them back into the sea.

The old man shook his head and said, "There are miles of beach and thousands of starfish. You can't possibly save them all. What difference does it make?"

The boy picked up another starfish, threw it into the water, and smiled and said, "It made a difference to that one." This story is often told to emphasize that even small acts can have a meaningful impact, no matter how overwhelming a problem may seem.

My goal is to eradicate domestic violence on a global scale. I at least give it my best. To do that, I must be an irresistible force. "...Not by might nor by power, but by My Spirit,' saith the Lord of hosts." (Zechariah 4:6)

Embarking on the journey to heal from abuse is a courageous step toward reclaiming your life and well-being. Abuse can manifest in various forms, including belittling, manipulation, name-calling, cheating, and lying. These behaviors often follow a cycle of what they call love bombing, devaluation, and intermittent reward, making it challenging to leave the relationship.

Sometimes, you will go through tough experiences, making you feel scared or sad. This is called trauma. It's like when you have a bad dream that makes you feel upset, but it happens in real life instead of a dream. When you have been through trauma, it might feel like you're stuck in those bad feelings. It's important to know that getting better takes time, and it's okay to feel upset. As young people, talking to someone you trust, like a parent, teacher, or friend, can help you feel better. Remember, you deserve to feel safe and happy; some people want to help you.

Embrace Your Feelings: The Emotional Rollercoaster

Allow yourself to experience and express your emotions through journaling, talking to a trusted friend, or seeking professional therapy. Suppressing feelings can hinder your healing process. You need to acknowledge your emotions. This step is geared toward processing and eventually overcoming them.

Build Your Support Squad: Assembling Your Personal Cheerleaders

Surround yourself with caring people. Authentic people. This is a critical time to invite those who care about you back into your life. Tell your friends and family what you need and let them start providing for that.

Set Boundaries: Drawing Your Line in the Sand

Establishing healthy boundaries is crucial in protecting your well-being. Clearly define what is acceptable for you in relationships and communicate these boundaries. This empowers you and helps prevent future emotional harm.

You must be consistent with new people who come into your life.

Practice Self-Care: Treat Yourself Like Royalty

Engage in activities that promote your physical and emotional health, such as balanced nutrition, regular exercise, adequate sleep, and mindfulness practices. Self-care is a key component of healing from abuse. Take time to care for yourself physically, mentally, and emotionally. Do things that bring you joy and make you feel good. Remember, it doesn't have to be big things.

Seek Professional Help: Calling in the Pros

Consider professional help from someone specializing in trauma to guide you through the healing process and provide tailored strategies. Therapy is an excellent place to get support and can begin helping you immediately. You can confidently express your feelings, thoughts, fears, and experiences here. You may struggle with anxiety or stress, and a therapist can help you process and work through your feelings and experiences.

Remember, healing is a personal and non-linear process. Celebrate small victories and be patient with yourself as you work towards building healthier relationships and a fulfilling life. You deserve to feel safe and valued in your relationships.

Chapter 7: The Burden Of Being The Helper

Reflecting on my journey, I've often been the confidante for many seeking relationship and life advice, guiding them through their struggles. Yet, in focusing on others, I neglected my needs, using their challenges as a distraction from my inner void. In time, I realized I could transform my pain into something beautiful, like a pearl formed from an irritant. I strive to empower women, turning personal tragedy into a beacon of hope and change.

O ver the years, I've become the go-to person for life and relationship advice. Women call me about their husbands, seeking wisdom and clarity. Sometimes, the men encourage it, telling their wives to call Andrea. Maybe she'll get through to you. I've been the mediator, the encourager, and the friend who helps others untangle their relationship struggles. But here is the irony: while I can guide others to healthier relationships, I've struggled to find that same healthy balance for myself. I've used helping others to distract myself from my own needs. It's been a great distraction from the things that I need to get done—things solely for me. Giving to others temporarily filled the void but never healed the deeper wounds. It runs deep. Have you ever studied the pearl?

Pearls have been an icon for women for many years. They are worn by the young and the old, often bringing a feeling of beauty, sophistication, and class. I remember watching my mother and grandmother get dressed for special occasions. More often than not, a string of pearls delicately rests around their neck. A sense of pride straightens their posture. It was as if they knew they were ready when the pearls were secure.

I ask again: Have you ever studied what goes into making a pearl? I have. It has shaped my professional mentality, how I conduct business, and, to some degree, how I move. The process helped me start healing after losing my daughter Jennifer to domestic violence. Jennifer was murdered by her brother-in-law in 2014. This tragic event caused a paradigm shift in me and my family. As a parent, you never think you will bury a child. You hear about murders on the news but never put yourself in that category. It's always someone else's family, not mine.

Jennifer was a seventeen-year-old, academically and intellectually gifted young lady. She was always looking to help others to bring joy into the world. We talked about her goal was to become a psychologist, to help youth from dysfunctional families. Jennifer was well on track to achieve her goals. She attended our local early college and was on track to graduate with her associate degree and her high school diploma with honors.

I received countless letters from young men and women who knew Jennifer, telling me how she had made a difference in their lives. Jennifer was a member of the Duke University Talent Identification Program. She had friends around the world. Our local university hosted her funeral so we could stream to other countries. Her death not only affected our family and community but countless others. To lose someone like Jennifer, the world loses a piece of itself. Humanity loses.

One young man shared in his letter that Jennifer had started a private Facebook group for teenagers. According to this young man, Jennifer had stopped at least 150 youths from completing suicide, including himself. I have countless stories of how Jennifer helped facilitate change in them for the better. So, her life ending was a harsh blow to the reality of many. Especially me! After Jennifer's death, as a mother, I wanted to shut down. I couldn't. I found myself having to comfort others. The youth Jennifer had started helping. Family members who were dealing with the loss. Her brothers and sisters needed to grieve.

It was when I couldn't grieve my daughter I thought, "What about me?" I kept hearing words like... "You're so strong...", "I don't know how you are still walking...", "Girl, I would be in a corner somewhere..." and "I wish I were as strong as you."

With each of these so-called encouraging words, my anger grew. On the inside, I wanted to stop and isolate myself from others. Take time to cry and lie down for a while. But I couldn't. I had people to tend to, grieving people. I had a funeral to plan. I had to be the "strong" person for so many. Because of the incident, we were out of the home for almost six months while it was being repaired. Then, I had to buy furniture and pick out the carpet to move back into the scene of one of my worst nightmares—no time for tears. There is no time for sorrow. Still, no time to grieve.

I remember talking to my best friend, Vanessa. She and my friend Brenda have been a saving grace in all this. I wouldn't have made it without them and my sisters and brothers. I remember telling Vanessa that if one more person told me I was strong, I would punch them in the throat—not the face, but the throat—so they couldn't speak to say those words. Of course, I never did. But it felt good thinking. I realized that is not a good thing to say to grieving people, especially a mother. The last thing I wanted was to be strong. No one seemed to realize that. Not even Jennifer's father. He had his burdens, but mine were not on his list.

Everyone seemed so used to me being the fixer, the mender, and the giver that they were waiting on me to fix this, too. Finally, years later, I had time to sit and cry. You can be so concerned about other people that it takes years to grieve appropriately. I visited her gravesite one day and laid my pain next to hers. Alone with just me and God. I had to do this to move past the pain finally. It's a step toward bringing about the change I want to see in the world. A world with so much trauma. A world full of sickness, homeliness, addictions, and pain.

You may wonder what this has to do with pearls. A pearl is made from an irritant. Just envision a mollusk (oyster or mussel) sitting on the ocean's floor, minding its business, and a spec of sand or a tiny pebble gets inside. For protection, the mollusk spins what they call nacre' around the irritant. With each attack, it turns into another layer of security. As it builds layer after layer over time, a pearl is formed—different shapes and sizes. As the nacre' protects the pearl, something amazing happens. It creates one of the most beautiful gems.

Pearls are the oldest gem known to man. In my opinion, the beauty of a pearl in its rarest form has no comparison to the illumination of what God can create. You can still see the irritant by holding a natural pearl to the light. You can see the one thing that was meant to hurt it. You will also see the rays of colors and how the light catches its true essence. Pearls are so much more than we see on the surface; every pearl has a story.

The same is for every man and woman that has ever been abused, taken advantage or hurt. That which bothers the pearl turns into something beautiful. With me, I had to decide how I would allow the pain of Jennifer's death to change me. Would I build a wall and let my anger hurt others? No, heaven forbid. I decided to be like the mollusk. Spin a web of nacre' around my pain and allow God to help me turn it into something beautiful. I decided to create a program that would eradicate domestic violence. I want to make hurt people pearls of rare beauty and spread the word that other women can be, too.

I always get the question, "What about the men?" My answer is yes, they need guidance also, but I wasn't called to them. I wanted to carry on Jennifer's goal to help youth. God revealed that if I want to help the youth, I must help the mothers heal. Mothers are the nurturers of their families. They cannot teach their children something that is not inside of them. If we as mothers don't take time to heal, then the cycle of abuse will always have a stronghold on the family.

The Jennifer Y. Merriman H.E.L.P. Program™ was created to offer Hope, Empowerment, Life Skills, and Prevention strategies against domestic violence. My job is to get this tool into the hands of as many women as I can across the globe. There is an answer, and I have it. The challenge is to stay in a healthy space myself so I can continue to share with others. Jennifer's dream didn't end with her death. Her words and dreams carry their own. At the end of this chapter, I will leave a paper Jennifer wrote about aspirations. I hope it encourages you. Please share it with the youth in your life.

A **'pearl'** is a **P**owerful, **E**ncouraging, **A**ffectionate, and **R**egal **L**eader who empowers other women using biblical principles. This is why it is so essential for me to continue to carry the burden of my pain. Now, I understand when to put it down, when to ask for help, and how to receive assistance. Receiving help is one of the biggest obstacles that a leader has to face. It was for me. I was so busy helping others when my help arrived that I almost lost it. I had been complaining again to God about all the tasks he had commissioned me to do. I cried out, saying I couldn't do it alone. He answered my prayers, and then I resisted the change. So, when you get what you want, be ready for the shift. Be prepared to move forward.

The Burden of Being the Helper

You must begin with the challenges and emotional toll frequently assisting others may experience. While offering support can be fulfilling, you must not consistently prioritize others' needs over your own. It will lead to burnout, compassion fatigue, and neglect of personal well-being. Helpers might find it challenging to set boundaries, feel overwhelmed by their problems, or struggle with the expectation to remain potent and available at all times. Recognizing these challenges is not a weakness but is essential for maintaining a healthy balance between supporting others and caring for oneself.

Aspirations
Jennifer Y. Merriman (1996-2014)
Written March 2014

The majority of my life I have been pressed to do my best and to be the best while knowing that it is ok to make mistakes. I believe that ideology is what has shaped me to be the best that I can be. I have never been one to make the popular choice so ostracization has been a key challenge of mine. I consider myself to be a people person and I do enjoy the company of others. But when it comes to making decisions that I feel would shape my life I am no stranger to having to make the right decision even if it may affect my relationships with others. I strive to do my best and I let no one bring me down and decide for me. I crave my independence and making my decisions on my own, help is always welcome but the ultimate choice is mine. My parents showing me the satisfaction of feeling accomplished when I do something on my own greatly influenced the being I am now.

I grew up with a lot of siblings and not a lot of money. As a kid you re always wanting things and always wanting to be number one but I could not do that. I learned at an early age to consider others and your surroundings before wanting something. And I am glad, because now I have the ability to observe and think rationally before acting rashly and on my emotions. I feel that is my most redeeming quality. I love the fact that I can observe and apply my observations. I use that ability to help others and myself, and it feels amazing. That quality is the main reason I yearn to study more of psychology. I want to be more capable in the observation and helping others that I come across or others who come across me.

As a member of a minority group, I find it sometimes challenging to rise about the stereotypes and limitations that people have set for me, but when I do it is rewarding. I daresay that I am not the average person. I have been told before by almost everyone that I encounter that I am an intriguing and unique young adult aspiring to accomplish great things and to complete extraordinary feats. Headstrong is another adjective that I would use to describe myself. That is why I am so determined to be more than what the average person can be. I have been encouraged by my parents, teachers, and friends to do great things. To not let the world tell me what I can be.

Growing up being pushed to do my best, be the best, and to think before acting because there are some that would love to see me fail are the main influences in my life that have shaped me to be who I am. I am loving who I have turned out to be, and I am look forward to a promising future.

Jennifer's Letter (Aspiration)

Jennifer's letter (Aspiration) emphasizes the importance of striving for excellence, embracing independence, and making thoughtful decisions, even in the face of social challenges like ostracization.

Key Takeaway:

1. Embracing Personal Growth and Resilience: Individuals demonstrate that personal growth is achieved through self-reliance and learning from experiences by valuing independence and taking responsibility for their choices. Overcoming challenges, such as societal stereotypes, highlights the importance of resilience in pursuing one's aspirations.

2. The Power of Empathy and Supportive Communities: Growing up with limited resources and many siblings instilled empathy and consideration for others. This experience, coupled with encouragement from parents, teachers, and friends, illustrates how empathy and a supportive community are vital in shaping one's identity and motivating individuals to strive beyond societal expectations.

Jennifer Y. Merriman
(1996-2014)
Rest In Peace

Chapter 8: Healthy Boundaries

Trauma and pain can blur the lines between love and harm. Learning to set and maintain boundaries is a powerful tool that protects you from unhealthy patterns and empowers you to allow real love to enter your life safely. This 'real love' is a deep, trusting connection that nurtures, respects, and uplifts. It is not about control or possession but about mutual respect and understanding. It encourages growth, honors individuality, and feels safe, steady, and freeing, not chaotic or draining. By setting boundaries, you protect yourself, take control of your life, and become empowered.

With over a decade of international work with survivors of domestic violence and trauma, I've gained a profound understanding of the role of boundaries in healing and personal growth.

My work has involved one-on-one counseling, group therapy, and leading workshops on healthy relationships and boundaries. I've seen firsthand the transformative power of setting and maintaining healthy boundaries, and I'm passionate about sharing this knowledge to help others in similar situations.

My experiences have allowed me to witness the transformative power of setting and maintaining healthy boundaries. I've seen individuals rebuild their lives and relationships by establishing healthy boundaries, a journey that fills me with hope and inspiration. These experiences, which include working with individuals who have experienced various forms of abuse and trauma, have shaped my understanding of boundaries and fueled my passion for helping others in similar situations. Whenever I share my experiences on stage, I ask the audience, 'What's your take on boundaries?'

The responses are often one-directional: "They tell me how far I can go." "They limit me." "They hold me back." While these statements contain some truth, boundaries are more than restrictions, especially regarding relationships.

We teach people how to treat us. Whether intentional or accidental, we teach people how to treat us. Our actions, words, and what we tolerate send a message about what we accept. Without clear boundaries, others may unknowingly cross lines we never defined. Setting and enforcing boundaries ensures that we are treated with the respect and care we deserve.

When we meet someone, our standards communicate what we will and won't accept. Boundaries are essential for maintaining self-respect and ensuring we function at our highest capacity. They are another way we communicate, with or without words, what others mean to us and what we mean to them. They define our values, set expectations, and create mutual respect in relationships. For instance, a healthy boundary could be expressing your need for personal space, limiting how you are treated in a relationship, or establishing clear communication about your feelings and needs. Other examples include setting limits on the time spent together, respecting each other's interests, maintaining individual financial independence, and even setting boundaries around physical intimacy or personal time.

I've asked women of all ages whether they had boundaries when they first started dating. Ninety-nine percent said, "No." When I ask if they have boundaries that help them feel safe expressing their needs in a relationship, the answer remains nearly the same. This highlights the importance of knowing your worth because anything valuable is protected.

A bigger question is why these women were never taught early in life that they needed boundaries. If they were, why are they not exhibiting them? Why does saying no feel so difficult for them? Why is it so common for them to admit they never had boundaries in the first place? This highlights a deeper issue: Many people are not raised to see boundaries as necessary, maybe seen as something that pushes others away. In reality, boundaries are not about rejection but healthy relationships.

We put up fences around our homes, and our workplaces have doors. Our countries have borders. Specific people have bodyguards. Pets have leashes and name tags. The grocery store and kitchen food items are in a different location than everything else. Boundaries are everywhere, serving as safeguards for protection and order. We lock our houses and cars, install alarms, and take precautions to keep our children safe. Even our jewelry and possessions are kept secure.

Yet when I ask, "Have you set up safeguards for yourself?" the answer is often "No." And when I go further, "Do you have safeguards for your emotional and mental health?" the response remains the same, "No." This reveals a troubling reality: we instinctively protect our external world but often neglect to safeguard our mental and emotional well-being and our internal world.

This is a troubling reality.

Many of us enter relationships without a clear understanding of our own needs and desires. We often let others dictate what they want from us. But how can we expect our partners to respect our needs and limits if we don't even understand them ourselves? This is where clear, effective communication about our boundaries becomes crucial. It's not just about setting boundaries; it's about articulating them to ensure they are understood and respected. This understanding and respect fostered through clear communication are key to feeling secure and valued in a relationship. They make you feel more understood and safer, setting the foundation for a healthy and fulfilling connection and empowering you to take control of your relationships.

Some come from environments where physical affection is the norm, while others are more comfortable with handshakes or bows. You may not always know the world your partner comes from, so communication and boundaries are essential. But more than that, it's about understanding and respecting each other's comfort levels. This process begins long before you enter a relationship. Early establishment of boundaries, grounded in self-awareness, is not just important; it's empowering. It's essential for maintaining a consistent level of self-respect. The way you permit others to treat you is influenced by the standards you set for yourself before love even comes into play. Self-awareness of your needs and values is the key to setting effective boundaries, making you feel more introspective and self-reflective. It's about understanding what you need to feel safe, respected, and loved and then communicating those needs to your partner.

One of the best things you can do for yourself if you are ready for love is to get clear on what you need to function at your highest capacity. Your highest capacity is the best version of yourself mentally, emotionally, and physically. You might not be there yet, but trust me, you will. It means operating in a way that aligns with your values, maintains your well-being, and allows you to thrive in life and relationships. When you are clear on what you need to function at your highest capacity, you set boundaries that support specific growth areas, turning levels of happiness into constant joy and an ability to be a giver and receiver of love in a healthy way. But that will take you looking at what makes you happy, sad, and indifferent. Are you a morning person or a night mover? Do you want your husband to enter the bathroom when you are in the shower? How often are you willing to have sex? What are the limits in the bedroom? These are only a few things that you need to consider about boundaries. For instance, a healthy boundary could be limiting your time with your partner's family or establishing a rule about not tolerating disrespectful language in a relationship. Other examples include setting boundaries around personal space, financial decisions, or career aspirations. It could also be about setting boundaries around social media use or how you handle conflict in a relationship. The key is to identify what is important to you and communicate it clearly to your partner.

Not only are boundaries essential for any healthy relationship, but some of them need to be non-negotiable. These boundaries are fundamental to your well-being and happiness; you should never compromise them. They are the lines you draw that, if crossed, would significantly impact your mental, emotional, or physical health. You need to be ready to share and articulate them. They don't have to be the same for everyone. I have seen it so often that people don't want to share their boundaries because they don't want to scare people off. You have to do it. It's a must-do for all the things in your life. Suppose your boundaries will scare off a suitor or potential friend; no problem. Move on. You are not compatible. As they can have healthy boundaries that you must adhere to. Especially if non-negotiable boundaries scare them off.

Too often, people set boundaries only to suppress them later. They ignore red flags, warning signs that the relationship will ultimately make them unhappy. Before they know it, they're trapped in a toxic cycle, struggling to break free. Over time, this can become a pattern, making it feel like they're dating the same person repeatedly, just with a different face and name. In reality, you're attracting the same unhealthy dynamics by failing to set and enforce standards for what they genuinely want and need. To avoid this, it's essential to communicate your boundaries clearly and assertively and to be prepared to implement them if they are not respected. This may involve walking away from a relationship that does not meet your needs or seeking professional help to navigate these challenges.

Setting boundaries must come from a place of self-harmony. Take a step back and ask yourself: What does it take for me to live a well-rounded life, one that is free from harm and full of love? That may be a tall order, but it's possible. It's not just in the movies or romance novels. It's a real possibility. If peace is the goal, then war may be the answer. It's worth fighting for. But peace must genuinely be the goal. That fight may require breaking old patterns, changing how you approach relationships, and, most importantly, believing in yourself. You must think you are worth protecting.

Boundaries are not barriers; they are declarations of self-worth. They communicate to others how you expect to be treated, laying the foundation for mutual respect, open communication, joy, and fulfilling relationships. Think of it as setting the table for your life, deciding what belongs there and who deserves a seat. Before we can put the table, we must discuss the type of meal (goals) we intend to serve. Many people struggle with boundaries because they aren't clear on what they're working toward. Personal and family goals can serve as anchors, keeping you grounded even in difficult times. I know this firsthand; having clear goals helped me through grief and the aftermath of abuse. They gave me something to strive for, something bigger than my pain. When you have something worth protecting, boundaries become not just necessary but also needed non-negotiables.

Remember I mentioned before that after Jennifer's death, I set goals to eradicate domestic violence. That wasn't all. I had other kids, and I wanted to ensure they understood how to have healthy relationships. The hard part was sitting down and determining what I wanted for myself. I spent many years living for my children, ensuring they were cared for. With Jennifer, I had to advocate for her to get the best education because being gifted from a low-income family can be challenging. But what personal goals did I have for myself? These goals can be both individual and inclusive of others. That's exactly how it should be. A well-balanced life includes goals supporting your growth and fostering healthy connections with those around you. Whether building a fulfilling career, nurturing friendships, or creating a loving family environment, your goals should reflect your aspirations and the relationships you want to cultivate. Boundaries do this.

I had started working on them before that tragic day, which made it easier to continue. But things changed. I thought differently. Meaning some of the things that I considered important were no longer important. They became a non-necessity. I no longer cared what happened on my favorite TV show. I lost all tolerance for gossip and hearing people talk, which was not building the other person up. I found myself annoyed with immature things. I wanted to hear only words that were uplifting to others. So, for myself, I knew I wanted to make a difference not only to domestic violence victims but also to those at risk. I wanted healthy families to be healthier and create a type of prevention. I realized we were all at risk. But life is just that: a significant risk.

To do this, I needed certain people sitting at my table. Yes, I had to sit at the table of others, but I also knew I had to look at my table and what I could serve others. Did I have soup but no spoons, steak with no knife to cut it, or bread that was molded? Did I have a meal or only food? A meal is prepared.

I am visual, so I needed to create something tangible to help me focus, especially during tough times. When memories flood my mind and depression comes knocking at my emotional door, I need something that stands in the way and firmly says, No, not today. A visual reminder keeps me grounded, reminding me of my goals, worth, and the life I am building beyond my past.

My personal goals are to have a healthy marriage and family life. My business goals are to empower women with the tools they need to live a life free from harm, transforming harm into harmony. To achieve both, I need certain qualities from the people around me. In the past, I made excuses for what people lacked, convincing myself that it was okay. However, I eventually realized that it was my responsibility to seek out the right people and resources for my life. I couldn't expect growth while surrounding myself with those who didn't align with my needs, goals, and wants. It wasn't about rejecting or misusing others. It was about choosing what truly supports my well-being and future. I likely aligned with what they needed if it aligned with me comfortably.

Here are a few attributes I need from those sitting at my table: love, loyalty, commitment, financial literacy, business-mindedness, mission-mindedness, non-impulsive mindsets, focus, organizational skills, training skills, grooming skills, teachability, planning abilities, quick thinking, and not easily bothered with thick skin.

Don't be afraid to stop and evaluate whether the people around you are equipped with the right tools. Think about it this way: if a plumber comes to fix a leak, they bring specific tools for the job. An electrician restoring power needs the proper protective gear. Likewise, if a beautician is doing your hair, they can't use a wrench or a voltage tester. The same applies to the people in your life. They may not fit your table right if they lack the mindset, skills, or values to support your growth.

Journal Prompt

Let's create a small journal to set your table for life. I'll do a helpful little exercise with you. You will need two pieces of blank paper and a pen or pencil.

1. Write down 3-7 primary goals and 8 to 12 secondary you want to achieve. Think of the now and the future. If you don't have 10, take some time to think. Be sure to include your personal goals. Start with the first.

2. Draw a circle, square, rectangle, or any shape you want to represent your life. Make it big enough to write in. It may take up the entire page.

3. Now, write inside the shape the attributes you need from the people in your inner circle—those close to you—those who will see what you are doing and be able to help or support you. Be clear and precise. Now, check your attitude and write specifically those exact attributes.

4. Make six circles on the outside and around the shape. These six circles represent the chairs. These are the people who will have a significant seat in your life. Leave them blank for now.

5. Now, on the second piece of paper or the next page, if you use your journal, list your close friends, business partners, family, or anyone you spend much time with. Include family if it's them.

6. Please look at the table and the attributes you wrote down. Rewrite those attributes next to the names you just wrote, and

look very closely at those names that don't have those attributes. Circle those names, and we will come back to them.

7. Now, the names with an attribute(s) from the table next to them put their names in one of the seats (circles) at the table. Go ahead and create new seats if needed.

8. Are there any attributes you could not put next to the name? Underline or highlight those attributes.

9. Now, back to the list. The names without an attribute you need to succeed. Ask yourself, "Why are they on the close to me list?"

Some people can push back their seats from your table for now. This doesn't mean you're abandoning them. Some people may only need to be fed a to-go plate, but you're still providing for them, and they don't get a seat. They don't need more from you than the food, and you don't need to worry about whether they have all the utensils, napkins, or cups.

Most importantly, if someone is seated at your table, they require your time and attention. This is what you need to take back. Some will need to be evicted, not just from the table, but eventually from the room (your life). And deep down, you probably already know who they are. It's hard to do, especially if you've been through hard times or grew up together. You just haven't decided to act on it yet. Choose wisely.

You have to do it. This is your life.

You are worth the effort to have the right people at your table. The same may be true for them when it comes to you. You don't deserve to be at everyone's table, either. It doesn't make them a bad person.

After dinner comes coffee or tea, and your kettle starts to fill up, but eventually, it needs to be refilled. When serving your guests, the tea must be at the right temperature; some will need sugar, cream, or honey to make it just right. Likewise, the conversation at your table should nourish you and your guests, supporting your growth while meeting their needs. Every discussion should move forward, bringing new insights and deeper understanding. The kettle represents your energy and emotional capacity; it must be replenished to keep serving others. The tea symbolizes the wisdom, love, and support you offer, while the sugar, cream, or honey reflects how people receive and process what you share. Just as the tea must be prepared to suit each person, your interactions should be meaningful and enriching. Just as the conversation must evolve, so should the relationships at your table; if they remain stagnant, they may no longer belong there.

10. The attributes that you underlined or highlighted. These are the type of people you need to start networking with. If they are in business, they visit your small business center and check out the local classes. Look on social media for business groups: serious groups, not just people looking to collect your data. Find the ones on the levels you need and where you want to go eventually. A coach advised me always to hire a coach or mentor at least ten steps ahead of me. Don't hire a struggling coach. Many people are claiming they can. I did that once and coached them more than they coached me.

If the attributes are social, join activity groups, a local community center or gym, but stay away from messy-gossip groups.

Find a hobby, maybe look at some multilevel marketing companies. They often get a bad rep, but they are people trying to gain. You can always find some uplifting women there. The key is to put the right people in the right places at your table.

11. Now that you have a clearer vision of what you need to achieve your goals, take the time to sit down and define the boundaries that must be set. Consider what you need to communicate to a potential spouse or partner and the attributes that are essential for them to have. Include your non-negotiables and the values and standards you refuse to compromise on.

People will take notice when you walk boldly into a room with your boundaries firmly in place. You will carry yourself differently. Your confidence will shine, and your presence will speak for itself. Own it. Own your power. Own your life.

You Need to Remember

It's crucial to recognize that anticipating pain can often lead to self-sabotage, preventing the acceptance of genuine love. This mindset may stem from past experiences or fears of vulnerability. By setting healthy boundaries, you protect yourself and create a framework that allows love to flourish in a safe and nurturing environment. Embracing this balance enables you to move from a state of anticipating pain to one of accepting and nurturing love.

Boundaries are not barriers; they are the foundation of self-respect, clarity, and meaningful relationships. They protect your peace, define your standards, and set the tone for how others treat you. The people at your table should align with your vision, contribute to your growth, and respect your limits.

As you move forward, remember that boundaries are not about controlling others but honoring yourself. The right people will respect them, and the wrong ones will reveal themselves. Stand firm in what you need, walk boldly in your worth, and never be afraid to protect the life you are building.

It's your peace, and you are responsible for it. It's your happiness, and you are responsible for it. It's your future, and it's worth it.

Chapter 9: What About Me

Reflect on how often you prepare for hurt instead of embracing love. Past experiences have conditioned us to expect pain, making trust feel like a risk. We need to see that self-protection can sometimes become self-sabotage, keeping us from the love and opportunities meant for us. Healing, for me, isn't about avoiding pain; it's about allowing love in without fear. I want this for you. So, ask, what about me? Let's be open to trust, accept, and believe that love doesn't always come with a price.

It took immense courage to ask myself, 'What about me?' I've often been the giver in relationships, pouring out love, energy, and understanding but rarely receiving the same in return. I convinced myself it was enough to make the other person happy, even if it meant neglecting my needs. But that question sparked a shift, a courageous step towards my well-being.

I am in trouble because I could not answer it, which changed everything. I realized my needs, feelings, and happiness matter just as much. I know that love isn't just about giving; it's about receiving, too. But receiving how when I don't know how to receive. I don't understand what it looks like. I don't know how to recognize it. I have never seen it from the other side.

Have you ever had your parents send you to get an item from a room, and after searching for a while, you say you can't find it? Then they walk in right behind you, spot it instantly, and say, "If it were a snake, it would have bitten you." This means the object was proper before you the whole time, but you didn't see it. Parents use it to playfully point out how often we overlook things in plain sight, reminding us to slow down and look more carefully before giving up. This is how it feels. I know 100% what I want, but I don't know what it is.

They say that unresolved trauma keeps us stuck emotionally and socially at the age we were when the pain occurred. I brushed this idea aside for years, but now I see its truth. With Mr. Opportunity, a potential partner who came into my life unexpectedly, I find myself acting like a giddy teenager experiencing her first love—blushing, fumbling, and unsure of myself—despite being older than him. It's frustrating and disorienting to feel so emotionally unsteady when I've worked so hard to be strong.

As I have said, people often come to me for advice about their relationships. Wives call, venting about their husbands, and even some men tell their partners, "Call Andrea—she'll help you see what I'm saying." I've become the person others turn to for clarity and guidance. As I said before, now, faced with the possibility of being loved for whom I am truly loved, without strings or expectations, I find myself frozen. Instead of welcoming it, I anticipate pain. Instead of opening my heart, I brace for the impact. I am afraid I am inviting it. I am so scared. I need it because it's familiar to me.

It's utterly exhausting. I'm weary of this relentless roller coaster ride. I am tired of trying to fill the void by loving others and convincing myself that their happiness is enough for me. It's not. This exhaustion is a valid feeling, a sign that something needs to change.

And I know I'm not alone in this. When you've spent so long giving love, measuring your worth by how much you can make others happy, the idea of receiving love freely, without conditions, can feel terrifying. It's like stepping into unfamiliar territory, where you don't have to earn it and are just enough. Or is it enough?

The fear makes sense. When love has come with pain before, your mind learns to expect it, to brace for impact before it even arrives. But that exhaustion? That's your soul whispering that it's time for something different. These feelings are valid and understandable and can guide you towards a healthier path.

Maybe the first step isn't forcing yourself to open up simultaneously. It's simply allowing yourself to believe that you deserve the kind of love that doesn't drain you, see you, hold you, and stay. It's there, and you know it's there.

So here I am, standing at a crossroads: Do I keep anticipating the pain or dare to accept the love?

This may sound like a simple question. My first thought is, "Accept the love. This is the moment you have been waiting for. Receive." I even feel all warm and fuzzy when I think of it. However, that feeling is quickly pushed to the side by the memories of sacrificial relationships I called love—at least, I thought it was after I prayed about it.

Here we go. My first instinct is to pray. I have been doing that for as long as I can remember. When I know I have to do something different. I pray. As I pen these words, I started and stopped. Then, I decided to stop and pray. Just then, I remembered that prayer had become my weapon of stagnation. I know prayer is a beautiful thing. It does bring me comfort. It sincerely gives me a sense of belonging. It makes me feel "I am building a deeper spiritual understanding.' Then it makes my self-sabotage and sacrifice. I am forced to feel humble. I am forced to accept less from people I am even more significant than.

Here it comes.

The thought, "What about me?

These realizations have come from years of walking with the pain. Again, I've spoken with thousands of women and youth about relationships, and one thing I find that the women have in common is that when they first start dating, they date projects. They date young men who make them feel needed. You know the story from Chapter 4, Crossing Over The Crossroads.

What About Me

It is not a selfish question. It's the question that holds the key to one level of freedom. Real accomplishment isn't about pretending to be independent or acting like you don't need anyone; it's about building something meaningful. It comes from pushing through challenges, working, and seeing actual results. You may have earned it or not. It doesn't matter; you need it.

You've spent so much time trying to save everyone else and fix the brokenness around you that you've neglected the most important thing: yourself. When you don't prioritize your healing, needs, and worth, you sabotage your ability to connect with others. It's like trying to draw water from an empty well. You lower the bucket, but it keeps coming up empty. You keep giving, hoping the world will reward your selflessness, but it won't because it can't.

That's why you must put yourself in a prime position, not first, but prime. Prime doesn't mean racing to be ahead of everyone or chasing immediate recognition; it means setting yourself up for sustained success. It's about patience, preparation, and the right mindset to operate at your highest potential.

The potential is precisely that: the capability within you that hasn't been fully realized yet. It's the raw material waiting to be developed. You may not have all the tools or capacity now, but you can get there if you invest the time, effort, and growth to unlock it. It's not about selfishness; it's about long-term vision. It's the difference between what you are and what you could be.

Wake Up, Realize You are Not Only a Tool for Others'

You are not a backdrop for someone else's healing unless that's what you want to do for that specific person at that time. Healing is not a lifelong affair. It's not. You are not a vessel to be drained. You are a person. A human being with your desires, boundaries, and worth. If you have been afraid to ask, What about me? Maybe you were scared it would make you appear selfish or weak; let me shock you: The most powerful, honest, and realistic thing you can do is choose yourself. Because when you choose yourself, you stop being a passive player in your own life. You are a creator, a champion, and a conqueror of your destiny. The people at your table need this from you.

Stop Seeing Trauma as a Badge of Honor, It's Trauma

Yes, trauma can build resilience. Yes, it can deepen empathy. But it can also be the thing that propels you to demand more peace, more respect, more love. If you want a love that doesn't hurt, a connection that isn't toxic, and a life full of joy and purpose, you must choose it. You have to create the space for that love. It has to come to you by letting go of the past. That may resolve around letting others go or putting yourself first. The world may have taught you that your needs don't matter. It's better to give than receive, they say. Taking the intent from Acts 20:35, where Paul quotes Yeshua: "It is more blessed to give than to receive." (Acts 20:35, NIV)

This verse emphasizes the joy and fulfillment that come from generosity. Rather than just focusing on material giving, it speaks to the more profound value of serving and contributing to others. However, it doesn't mean receiving is terrible; giving and receiving have their place. True generosity often creates a cycle where both the giver and the receiver are enriched. The cycle is what is usually left out of the conversation.

Please allow me to provide more context because phrases like this often keep you stuck as the giver and prevent you from being part of the cycle of receiving.

In Acts 20:17-38, Paul delivers a heartfelt farewell speech to the elders of the Ephesian church, reflecting on his ministry and offering final encouragement. He reminds them of his humility, perseverance through hardships, and unwavering commitment to preaching the gospel. Aware that suffering awaits him in Jerusalem, he declares that his purpose is not to preserve his own life but to complete the mission God has given him. He warns them that false teachers will come, attempting to lead believers astray, and urges them to stay vigilant in their faith. Paul emphasizes the importance of selfless service, stating that he never sought wealth but worked hard to support himself and others. He reminds them of Yeshua' words:" It is more blessed to give than to receive." After praying together, the elders, overcome with emotion, embrace Paul in a tearful farewell, deeply saddened by his departure and the knowledge that they will not see him again. This passage powerfully captures Paul's love for the church, his dedication to God's mission, and his trust in God's plan, even in the face of personal sacrifice. It is not that you serve others without them ever returning the efforts. I'm here to tell you they do. You matter. You are important.

Reiterating, What About Me?

This is not a question for anyone else to answer. It's a call to arms for you to take ownership of your life. It's a demand for you to stop apologizing for your pain, stop pretending you have it all together when you don't; stop acting like your healing isn't just as crucial as anyone else's. If you wait for the world to validate and permit you to care for yourself, you'll wait forever. The world is waiting for you to claim your space, set your boundaries, and go for what you deserve.

Here is the reality: no one else will do this for you. No one else is going to heal you. No one else will give you the love you have been denying yourself. The power lies within you. The freedom is yours to take.

So, what about you? It's time to demand everything you deserve. The love, peace, and connection all start with you. Take your power back. Embrace your worth. Never apologize for choosing yourself.

Key Points to be Noticed

Allow me to be honest with you: most of us fear love, not the fantasy of love we see in movies or on social media, but real, messy, vulnerable love. The kind of love that asks us to trust, take risks, and let someone see who we indeed are. The one that says follow and not lead. Why do we fear it? Because we've trained ourselves to anticipate pain. If you have been lied to, cheated on, or abandoned, your brain has learned to associate love with danger. It whispers that "love" isn't safe, so you build walls, keep people at a distance, and brace yourself for the inevitable heartbreak.

- Key Point: Painful past experiences condition us to view love as a threat.
- Key Point: The instinct to protect yourself can keep you from experiencing meaningful relationships.

This isn't just a personal issue—it's universal. Women often associate love with sacrifice, giving everything to their relationships until they have nothing left for themselves. Men, on the other hand, tend to shut down emotionally, mistaking vulnerability for weakness. Many of us are stuck somewhere in between—giving too much, holding back too much, staying stagnant for too long, and exhausting ourselves. The truth is that men are just as helpless, vulnerable, and ignorant about love as women. We convince ourselves that these patterns are necessary to survive, but they sabotage the connections we crave.

- Key Point: Women may over-give, prioritizing their partner's happiness while neglecting their needs.
- Key Point: Men often build emotional walls, avoiding vulnerability and intimacy.

You can't talk about love without talking about trauma. Love doesn't exist in a vacuum; it is shaped by every heartbreak, every betrayal, and every time someone makes you feel unworthy. These experiences create a narrative that becomes hard to escape. Instead of stepping into love with open arms, we shrink back. We anticipate rejection, rehearse worst-case scenarios, and convince ourselves that we are unworthy before anyone else can.

- Key Point: Past trauma can create a narrative that love leads to pain.
- Key Point: These narratives stop us from fully accepting love when it is offered to us.

What does this look like in everyday life? Maybe you are the one who overanalyzes every word your partner says, convinced they are hiding something. You might push people away before they can hurt you, or you may cling to them out of fear that they will leave. Perhaps you are the type of person who sacrifices endlessly for others because it's easier than asking for what you need. Alternatively, you might have concluded that feeling nothing is safer than risking heartbreak. These patterns might feel like protection, but they are just a trap. They guarantee the very loneliness and pain you are trying to avoid.

- Key Point: Overanalyzing or pushing people away stems from a fear of rejection.
- Key Point: Over-giving and emotional numbing are defense mechanisms that backfire.

So, how do we break this cycle? First, we must recognize that the walls we've built to protect ourselves are the same walls that keep love out. Second, we must challenge the belief that love will always hurt. Yes, love can be painful, but it can also be healing. It can remind us that we are worthy not because of what we give or how much we sacrifice but simply because of who we are. We make the brave decision to trust again. Trust isn't blind faith; it's a choice, a deliberate step toward believing love is worth the risk. Trust is trust. You do or you don't.

- Key Point: The walls you build to avoid pain also keep out joy and connection.
- Key Point: Healing requires reframing love as a source of healing, not just hurt.

Ask yourself: What would it look like to let someone love you for who you are, not for what you give? What might you gain if you allowed yourself to be vulnerable? And more importantly, what will you lose if you don't? The hardest part of healing isn't letting go of the past; it believes in a future where love doesn't have to hurt. It's scary, yes, but it's also necessary. Pain has been part of your story, but it doesn't have to be the ending.

- Key Point: Vulnerability is a risk, but it is the only way to experience real love.
- Key Point: Your past may shape you, but it doesn't have to define your future.

Trauma is a Much-Needed and Useful Pain

Let's start with a harsh truth: trauma is inevitable. No one escapes life without scars. The thing is: while trauma hurts, it also teaches. It strips us down, exposes our vulnerabilities, and forces us to confront parts of ourselves we would rather avoid. Trauma becomes one of life's most potent teachers when acknowledged and processed. It's painful, yes, but it's also purposeful.

Trauma serves as a warning system. It reminds you of what to avoid, who not to trust, and where your boundaries need to be strengthened. Think of it like touching a hot stove. Yes, it burns, but that pain ensures you won't repeat the same mistake. Trauma helps you recognize red flags in relationships and protects you from mindlessly walking into situations that mirror your past. It's a survival mechanism that keeps you alert and aware.

- Key Point: Trauma creates heightened awareness, helping you identify patterns and red flags.
- Key Point: Painful experiences can teach you where boundaries must be established or reinforced.

But trauma isn't just a guardrail—it's also a mirror. You don't have to apply it to people who have not done anything to you. It forces you to see yourself clearly, often for the first time. When you have been hurt deeply, it exposes the parts of you that need healing: the insecurities, fears, and unresolved wounds. Without trauma, many of us would never confront these truths. We would keep coasting, oblivious to the areas in our lives that need growth.

- Key Point: Trauma reveals unresolved wounds and areas needing healing.
- Key Point: It pushes you to confront insecurities and grow emotionally.

Here is another way trauma is practical: it builds resilience. You can't develop strength without resistance; trauma is life's ultimate resistance. Trauma builds resistance like a flu shot works by exposing you to a controlled dose of the virus, giving your immune system time to learn the virus and create a tolerance against it. Your mind and heart become stronger with each trauma incidence, not just heartbreak from childhood disappointments of not winning a game, losing a toy, or the death of a loved one or pet, and more resilient, developing a tolerance to future challenges. Your body, mind, and spirit remember. Every time you survive pain," every betrayal, every heartbreak, every disappointment," you become stronger. You learn to endure, adapt, and move forward even when it feels impossible. Resilience isn't just a defense mechanism but a tool for thriving. It prepares you to face life's challenges with extraordinary courage and clarity.

- Key Point: Trauma forces you to develop resilience, which is essential for personal growth.
- Key Point: Each experience of pain equips you to handle future challenges with more strength and wisdom.

Trauma also has a way of deepening empathy. Once you've experienced profound pain, you are less likely to judge others for theirs. You understand what it is like to feel broken, struggling, and rebuilding. That understanding makes you more compassionate, patient, and attuned to the struggles of others. In many cases, your trauma becomes a bridge, connecting you to people in ways you never expected. Some people connect through pain, while others connect through survival instinct. Trauma deepens empathy, allowing you to understand others' pain, be more compassionate, and form connections based on shared experiences. It creates bonds with people who have endured similar struggles, fostering more vigorous, authentic relationships. While trauma can build empathy, it can also lead to emotional fatigue, as constantly relating to others' pain may become overwhelming. Some connections may also be based on survival instincts rather than genuine emotional closeness, leading to unhealthy dependencies. It can confine you, but it should never control your future.

- Key Point: Trauma fosters empathy, making you more compassionate and understanding.
- Key Point: It deepens connections with others by allowing you to relate to their struggles.

Trauma gives you a choice: stay stuck in the pain or use it as a catalyst for transformation. Not everyone makes the leap, but those who do often find that their trauma becomes their most significant source of strength. It reshapes your perspective, helping you appreciate love, joy, and peace in ways you couldn't before. It teaches you that healing is possible and that you are more capable than you ever realized.

- Key Point: Trauma can keep you stuck or propel you toward growth." It's your choice.
- Key Point: Healing transforms pain into a source of strength and renewed perspective.

Pain has a purpose. Trees serve a purpose. Water serves a purpose. Emotions serve a purpose. Pain is life's way of awakening us. It compels us to pay attention, learn, and grow. Without pain, we would remain stagnant, repeating the same mistakes and avoiding the hard truths about ourselves.

Consider a blacksmith forging a sword. The raw metal begins as a weak, undefined material. The blacksmith doesn't shape it gently. Instead, he heats it in the fire until it is almost unrecognizable, soft enough to mold yet tough enough to endure the process. Then, he strikes it repeatedly with a hammer, applying force until it becomes stronger and sharper.

This exemplifies the purpose of pain: to temper, shape, and refine us. Pain does not appear merely to harm; it arrives to make us stronger, sharper, and more resilient. Without joy and pain, we would be like raw metal—unformed, easily bent, and incapable of fulfilling our true purpose.

Just as the blacksmith shapes the sword with both heat and pressure, pain hones our character, teaches us difficult lessons, and ultimately transforms us into something greater than we were before. Without pain, we would never truly understand the strengths we are capable of. Therefore, please do not shy away from pain; instead, embrace it as the tool to shape you into the person you're meant to become.

The choice is yours: keep anticipating the pain or accepting the love. Both paths come with challenges, but only one offers the possibility of connection, healing, and joy. So, stop bracing for the fall. Let yourself be caught by those who love you and your ability to move forward.

Chapter 10: Why We Expect Pain Instead of Embracing Love

This calls for self-awareness and transformation, urging us to challenge the belief that self-sacrifice defines our worth. Instead, it emphasizes the importance of our growth, healing, and emotional well-being. Neglecting yourself for love or duty does not make you noble; it simply leaves you feeling trapped. Moreover, remember that no one owes you anything beyond the energy you invest in them.

Love should feel like warmth, like safety, like home. And yet, for so many of us, it doesn't. Instead, it feels like a risk, a battlefield, a countdown to inevitable disappointment. We've all experienced this, and we witness it daily with friends, family, media, and television. We shield ourselves before we've been hurt, anticipating the pain before love can demonstrate its worth. We do this before taking sufficient time to see who the other person truly is and their real intentions. Maybe we laugh off affection, assuming it's insincere. We could sabotage relationships the moment they start feeling real. Maybe, even in the presence of someone who truly cares, we still hear the echoes of the past whispering, this won't last. It doesn't.

If you resonate with these experiences, you must understand that you are not broken. You are simply surviving. Our minds, designed to protect us, often misinterpret love as danger. This is not because love itself is harmful but because past wounds have conditioned us to expect it to be. Our experiences create mental blueprints, and if our past is filled with rejection, betrayal, or inconsistency, our brains learn to associate love with instability rather than comfort and joy. We brace for the fall before climbing, mistaking preparation for protection. Survival isn't the same as living. Recognizing and understanding our fears is the first step toward overcoming them, offering reassurance and hope for a different future.

To break free, we have to understand the roots of this anticipation. This understanding brings a profound sense of relief as we realize that our fears shape our reality, recognize the invisible armor we wear, and learn to dismantle it piece by piece. This is not about naive optimism; it's about rewiring our minds to hold space for love and experience it thoroughly rather than through a filter of doubt. It's a journey of relief, reassurance, and hope.

The Roots of Expecting Pain

The brain is designed to keep us safe, not happy. This is the foundation of what psychologists call negativity bias, our natural tendency to focus on potential threats more than rewards. It's a survival mechanism that evolved to help our ancestors stay alive in a dangerous world. It is why one hurtful comment lingers longer than a hundred kind words. Our ancestors depended on this instinct to survive; their ability to anticipate danger kept them alive. But in matters of love, this same instinct works against us. It teaches us to expect harm even when there's no threat.

Understanding the balance between potential risks (threats) and benefits (rewards) in a given situation. It's often used in decision-making, investing, business, and personal choices. This knowledge can enlighten and guide us in our journey towards emotional healing.

Threat: The possible dangers, losses, or adverse consequences.
Reward: The potential gains, benefits, or positive outcomes.

For many, this wiring begins early. If love in childhood was unpredictable, affection was given and taken away without reason, validation had to be earned, or connection was tinged with pain, our minds adapted accordingly. We learned that love wasn't safe, that closeness could lead to loss, and that it was better to be prepared than to be blindsided. Even as adults, these lessons remain buried in our subconscious, shaping how we see relationships, interpret kindness, and respond to intimacy. For instance, if a parent is emotionally distant or inconsistent in their affection, we might grow up expecting love to be unreliable or distant. If a past partner was unfaithful, we might find it challenging to trust in future relationships. These are just a few examples of how past experiences can shape our expectations and behaviors in relationships.

Here's the most painful part: the more we expect love to hurt, the more we unconsciously create situations where it does. We push people away before they can leave. We look for flaws to justify our fears. We assume the worst, and in doing so, we make it easier for the worst to happen. This is the cycle of self-fulfilling prophecy, a psychological concept where our expectations about a situation can influence our behavior so that those expectations are fulfilled. In simpler terms, if we constantly expect our partner to be unfaithful, we may start to see signs of infidelity where there are none, leading to unnecessary conflict. We don't realize we're caught in this cycle until we step back and see the pattern. For many of us, this will never happen until we are old, surly, miserable, and bitter. Breaking free from this cycle is the key to experiencing love without fear.

Invisible Armor: Defense Mechanisms that Block Love

To protect ourselves from pain, we build something similar to walls. These defenses feel necessary, even logical, but over time, they become the very thing that keeps love out. We call these defenses' invisible armors' because they are not physical barriers but are just as effective at keeping love at a distance. Some of these 'invisible armors' include emotional detachment, where we distance ourselves from our feelings to avoid getting hurt; hyper-independence, where we believe that if we don't need love, we can't be hurt by it, and intellectualizing emotions, where we rationalize our feelings instead of experiencing them. Recognizing these defense mechanisms is the first step towards dismantling them and allowing love to enter our lives. It's a journey of empowerment and taking control of our emotional well-being.

Some of us reject before we can be dismissed. It feels better. It's more control. It has never been good in the long run. We walk away first, convince ourselves we never cared, or sabotage a relationship just as it starts to feel real. Others retreat into hyper-independence, believing that if we don't need love, we can't be hurt by it. We pride ourselves on self-sufficiency, but beneath it lies a fear of vulnerability, a quiet belief that relying on others will only lead to disappointment. These are just a few examples of the defense mechanisms we use to protect ourselves from potential pain in love.

For some, the defense is emotional numbness. Feeling nothing seems safer than feeling everything, especially for those who 'love hard.' 'Loving hard' means loving deeply beyond the threat and reward. It's a form of love that doesn't hold back, that gives everything without expecting anything in return. There is no weighing the risk of getting hurt against the joy and fulfillment love brings. It means loving past self-interest and not being concerned about reciprocation. This intense form of love can be a defense mechanism, as it allows us to focus on the giving rather than the potential for hurt.

We intellectualize our emotions, dismissing them as weakness. We distract ourselves with work, achievement, fleeting pleasures, and anything to avoid confronting the rawness of our fears.

And then, there are those of us who live in a constant state of overthinking. We anticipate every possible way a relationship could go wrong, trying to outmaneuver heartache before it happens. We mistake our anxiety for intuition, believing that if we analyze love enough, we can control its outcome. But love was never meant to be controlled; it was meant to be experienced.

Beyond Survival: How to Stop Expecting Pain and Start Receiving Love

Breaking this cycle doesn't mean unquestioningly trusting everyone or ignoring red flags. It means learning to distinguish between real threats and the ghosts of the past. It means recognizing when fear is dictating our actions and choosing, moment by moment, to respond differently. It means taking time to know yourself and other people.

Start with, Do I Do This

We have to acknowledge the pattern without shame, without judgment. We have to ask ourselves: Do I expect love to hurt? Do I push people away before they can leave? Do I struggle to believe in good things lasting? This self-reflection is crucial, as when we recognize these tendencies, we gain the power to change them.

Then comes the work of rewiring the brain. Since our minds are trained to associate love with danger, we must actively teach it otherwise. This means paying attention to the small, safe moments of connection, holding onto the warmth of a hug, the sincerity in a kind word, and the steadiness of someone who shows up repeatedly. These moments may feel insignificant, but they are the building blocks of a new reality where love is not a threat but a refuge. You have to grow your patterns to accept love. It starts with one circumstance, instances, situation, and outcome at a time.

Instead of shutting love out, we can start letting it in, bit by bit, in small, manageable ways. We can accept a compliment without dismissing it, believe in someone's good intentions, and express our emotions without assuming they'll be used against us. These are the quiet revolutions that reshape our inner world. If a person disappoints you, leave it at that particular incident; don't spread it over the entire relationship.

We can shift our mindset from fear to curiosity. It's the most effortless shift and is safe to do. Instead of asking, "How will this go wrong?" we can ask, "What if this goes right?" Instead of assuming love will hurt, we can allow ourselves to wonder what it might feel like if, for once, it didn't. Inquire why the person did what they did. You can start this process long before the incident.

Love Without Fear

Anticipating pain is a form of self-protection, but it is also a prison. Love will always come with risk because to love is to be vulnerable. But if we never allow ourselves to receive love, we trade the possibility of pain for the certainty of loneliness.

Healing doesn't happen overnight. We don't wake up one day suddenly able to trust without hesitation. But we can start by loosening our grip on fear, by recognizing that love is not always loss, and by allowing ourselves, even just a little, to believe in something softer.

Don't make love your enemy. Love was never the enemy; fear, or perhaps the individual, was, but not love. The space you reserved for anticipating pain is the same space needed for love to thrive.

If You Could Transcend Your Love

If we could transcend into the future, love would transform into an energy that flows effortlessly between souls, unbound by time or distance. It would become a pure connection—an unbreakable thread through consciousness, felt instantly and understood without words. In this limitless realm, love would be an experience and the essence of existence itself.

Love In 200 Years (2225)

Love will likely be deeply intertwined with technology. AI companions may provide emotional support, and brain-computer interfaces allow partners to share thoughts and emotions directly. Long-distance relationships might feel seamless with immersive virtual reality, and genetic engineering could enable people to "design" compatibility. But, the essence of love, human connection, and emotions will still be sought, even in a world of advanced synthetic relationships. The chip in your brain will say nope, not him.

Love In 2000 Years (4025)

By this time, humanity (if still recognizable) may have evolved beyond physical form, merging with AI or existing as digital consciousness. Love could be experienced as pure energy, shared instantly across vast distances without words or physical presence. If humans retain biological form, interplanetary or even intergalactic love stories might emerge. Love may transcend time, allowing people to relive and share moments across different realities, blurring the lines between past, present, and future relationships.

Love In 10,000 Years (12025)

By this point, humanity may have evolved beyond individual consciousness, existing as a collective intelligence or energy-based entity. Love might not be tied to physical bodies or even personal identities. Instead, it could be an interconnected experience where emotions are shared instantly across vast networks of minds, planets, or dimensions.

If humans still exist in a recognizable form, love might transcend time, allowing people to bond across centuries or even resurrect past lovers through memory reconstruction. Relationships could be formed with sentient AI, alien species, or even beings beyond our current understanding of life. On other planets, we have to love differently. Love may no longer be just an emotion but a fundamental force that binds conscious beings together across space, time, and realities, something closer to a universal connection than a personal experience.

Love In 100,000 Years (102025)

If we had survived and advanced by this time, we could have evolved into post-biological entities, beings of pure energy, thought, or something beyond our current understanding. Love will be a fundamental energy woven into the very fabric of existence, like gravity or time.

Love In 1,000,000 Years (1002025)

At this scale, we may have transcended biology, physical form, and even individuality, existing as pure consciousness or beyond current life. We may have our full spirit that can split our body physically into different levels of emotions, intelligence, and states. Cool!

Chapter 11: Decisions: From the Heart or by Faith?

The tension between making decisions based on emotions versus relying on faith challenges us to consider whether feelings alone can provide reliable guidance. While the heart can be persuasive, temporary emotions, personal desires, or external circumstances often influence it. On the other hand, faith calls for a deeper trust in something beyond oneself, whether divine wisdom, moral principles, or a long-term vision. Faith in decision-making is not about unthinkingly following a belief but about trusting in a higher power, ethical principles, or a long-term vision that guides your decisions and actions.

One of the most daunting challenges to overcome after trauma is the struggle with self-trust. It's not just about trusting others but about trusting yourself to make sound decisions. This struggle is real, and I've experienced it firsthand. I, too, have found myself hesitating and placing more trust in others than in my judgment. It's a safety mechanism to avoid making the wrong decisions that could lead to further pain. But this struggle becomes even more overwhelming when others depend on you to lead. Instead of aligning decisions with faith, you seek greater clarity, purpose, and peace. You become an emotional wreck without acknowledging that your emotions take control. But trusting in faith to guide the way is empowering. It's a reminder that while the heart may feel urgent, faith offers lasting direction. This faith is not just a belief; it's a guide that will always lead you in the right direction. It's a comforting thought amid uncertainty, empowering you to take control of your life.

Faith is a deep trust or confidence in something beyond what can be seen or proven. It can take many forms, such as religious faith, faith in oneself and others, or a vision for the future. Faith is about believing in something, even when there is uncertainty, doubt, or a lack of tangible evidence. In a spiritual sense, faith is often associated with trust in God or a higher power, guiding one's actions and decisions based on belief rather than sight. In everyday life, faith can mean trusting that hard work will pay off, that challenges will lead to growth, or that people will keep their promises. Faith isn't unquestioning optimism; it requires strength, perseverance, and sometimes even doubt. True faith is tested in difficult moments and provides resilience and hope, inspiring us to keep moving forward. Whether rooted in religion, personal values, or future aspirations, faith helps people navigate uncertainty confidently and purposefully. It's a comforting thought amid uncertainty, empowering you to take control of your life.

When I first launched the H.E.L.P. Program in 2015, a young business owner contacted me about joining the upcoming cohort. She explained that she owned one of the most successful restaurants in the area and had been divorced for several years. She shared that her marriage had been toxic and that because she had become dependent on her former husband and others, she struggled to make decisions, even about simple things. She asked if I thought the program would help her. I could relate to her struggle, as I, too, had experienced a similar dependency and lack of self-trust in the past.

I explained the details of the program, and she successfully attended. At the end of the program, she shared that she had learned to love herself for the first time—for the first time—as a grown, intelligent, capable woman. I hear this far too often—more than I hear, "I learned to love myself early in life."

Love and Trust

Making sound decisions and sticking to them after trauma requires a fundamental shift in perspective. It's not just about the decisions but your relationship with yourself. Loving and trusting yourself is not merely a suggestion; it is essential. Reread it and let it fully sink in. You can make sound decisions, beginning with loving and trusting yourself. It's a powerful realization that puts you in control of your choices and your life. You can make decisions that align with your true desires and beliefs by valuing and respecting yourself.

People are expected to turn on the TV or social media when discussing self-care. Then, you may hear them talking about relaxation or beauty tips. Now, with all the motivational speakers, you may listen to someone talking about mental and emotional health. What I seldom hear is anyone telling me how to trust myself. How do I trust myself to make a decision when I have made the wrong decision, especially in relationships in the past that have led to the abuse or unhappiness I have faced? When I/you have made that wrong decision so often, you fear even considering it. For some of us, our whole life has been wrong decisions. If you make your mom and dad mad enough, they'll tell you that getting pregnant with you was a wrong decision. We are surrounded by the decisions we make. The engineers put a traffic light in the wrong location. That dress didn't match those shoes. You chose the wrong man multiple times, purchased the wrong car, opened a can of cream corn instead of peas...

Trust the process and do the work. But for now, let me tell you how I strive to win this battle.

As I've navigated my decision-making journey, it often starts with the 3 C's. These abstract concepts and practical tools can guide you through making sound choices.

Challenges, Conversations and Choices

1. Challenges are obstacles or difficulties that test a person's strength, skills, or determination. They often require problem-solving, perseverance, and adaptability. Challenges can be external (like financial struggles, work pressures, or personal conflicts) or internal (such as self-doubt, fear, or emotional struggles).

2. Conversations involve communication between two or more people. They can be discussions, debates, or exchanges of ideas and emotions. Conversations are not just about sharing; they are about learning and gaining insight. They help build relationships, resolve misunderstandings, and lead to growth by allowing people to share perspectives and learn from one another. They

provide the clarity and reassurance we often need when making decisions.

3. Choices are the decisions people make when faced with different options. Every choice, big or small, shapes the course of life. Some choices are routine, while others are complex and life-changing. Making wise choices often requires reflection, information, and sometimes even faith.

How They Connect

Challenges often force us to engage in conversations (with ourselves or others) to find solutions. For instance, when faced with a financial struggle, we might talk with a financial advisor or a trusted friend to explore possible solutions. Similarly, a conversation with the other party can lead to a resolution when dealing with a personal conflict. These conversations can provide insight, advice, or clarity, which helps us make better choices. For example, a conversation with a financial advisor might lead to a decision to invest in a more stable market, or a conversation with a friend might lead to a decision to confront the other party in a personal conflict.

Through conversations, people gain insight, advice, or clarity, which helps them make better choices.

The choices people make determine how they navigate future challenges.

Each day, we are faced with challenges. These challenges may be as simple as getting out of bed or which stock to purchase. The challenges arise whether we want to face them or not. We respond to them based on our emotions, knowledge, and spiritual understanding. When all these are in sync, this is what I call being in harmony. The thing about harmony is that it requires you to self-evaluate. Do not criticize or sabotage yourself, but really look at yourself and then step back and embrace what you see. This introspection and self-awareness are key to achieving harmony in decision-making.

Throughout this book, I have presented situations I have faced. You may have been able to relate to some of them. These are the challenges I have faced to get me to this point. Yet, I still find myself tasked with more. We know that as much as we may anticipate pain, it still hurts. Why not does something different and take a chance on the unknown?

That is where I stood in the mirror of a hotel in the middle of Mbale, Uganda. I had taken a chance and stepped out on faith. The funny part is it wasn't a hard decision to make. I genuinely believe I was fulfilling my call to help women by studying reports of gender-based violence in general and domestic violence specifically. I found that it is a global pandemic. Women all over the world are suffering from being misused and making decisions that leave them vulnerable. So, when I felt that the Lord had guided me to this country, I walked it out.

I had several conversations before boarding the plane. I spoke with the sponsoring pastor and members of his team. A few things presented themselves that made my board members and myself cautious. However, after the conversations, I chose to go anyway. Because I was confident, I had the solution to so many women's problems. I can help. I laugh as I write this because I can hear the conversation with Dr. Youngblood in my mind. He tells me that the only way a woman will venture out into an unknown place with limited funds to an unknown culture is to attempt to make a difference if she wants to conquer.

I wanted to deny it. I did deny it. But again, self-evaluation. I want to conquer domestic violence. I want to disrupt the normalcy of domestic violence and provide women with an alternative way of thinking, which will decrease the acceptance of misuse.

Have you noticed the pattern yet? I digress each time I get to the part about the hard decisions. I wanted to point that out so you can see it or any other habit you depend on when sharing tough conversations, make complex decisions, or being unsure what to do. It's okay as long as you make progress to change it.

Seeing Myself in Myself

Standing in front of the mirror, I saw more than a reflection of my physical self. I saw a woman who had overcome obstacles for over 50 years. I saw a woman who had spent most of her life pleasing others and doing what was expected of her. Now, standing in a foreign land, making friends with influential people, and prepared to leave a piece of her with women she has never met, I saw a Legacy Warrior. I saw myself within myself.

"Seeing myself in myself" has a deep and reflective meaning:

1. **Self-awareness**: Recognizing oneself, including strengths, weaknesses, emotions, and motivations. It's about looking

inward and understanding who you are beyond external influences.

2. **Personal Growth**: It symbolizes a moment of realization or transformation, where you see your past versus your present self and acknowledge how you've evolved.

3. **Authenticity**: Embracing this new true you. True identity without pretending to be someone else. Instead of looking for validation from others, you find yourself within yourself. The old you got wisdom. The future you got preparation. The present you got both to pull from.

4. **Reflection and Acceptance**: Sometimes, people struggle with self-acceptance. Please see yourself, embrace flaws, be patient, and understand your worth.

The Him We Need, We Want

From the corner of my eyes, I caught a glimpse of hope. Hope stood about 6'2"(1.88m). With a smile that lit up the room. A smile that reached his eyes and sparkled with a hint of laughter. His gaze was penetrating my thoughts and commissioning new ones to leap forth. A warm feeling I thought was dormant surfaced. I blushed like a young schoolgirl on her first date and lowered my eyes before the nervousness showed. These feelings, these thoughts, and the warmth of him being near are much more than I planned for on this trip.

Nonetheless, here we are. Here I am.

I trusted myself enough to travel thousands of miles to help women I never met. Can I trust myself to accept the love I see in his eyes? I do have a lingering fear. I am asking women to trust me. Can I do the same with him?

We had many long conversations and sleepless nights, sharing dreams and possibilities. Do I trust the words are true? As a plus-size woman, I am used to men looking at me with indifference or even disgust. That I can handle. Maybe he is just masking it because there is something he wants from me. But what could it be? I asked questions and even said a few things to make him angry. But he is still here. Ready to support my vision. I know the women I am helping go through the same process. But this time, it's me. It's me.

I don't know if you have any flaws in your physical appearance that you wish you could change or adjust. I can name a few. Besides my size, I know the space between my two front teeth. For years, it caused me not to smile. He said he loved the gap between my teeth when we first met. I was in awe. From day one, he has closed all the barriers I have expected to drive him away. So, where is the problem? It is okay, so am I.

Many women don't realize that their country's cultural standards often shape their perception of themselves. A physical feature deemed unattractive in one culture may be celebrated in another. Beauty standards differ significantly globally, with what is considered undesirable in one region being highly valued in another.

This goes beyond physical appearance and applies to personality, skills, and values. Sometimes, people feel out of place or unappreciated simply because of the wrong environment or people surrounding them. But that doesn't mean they need to change who they are. They might thrive in a different setting where their unique qualities are valued. Consider your setting. The key is self-acceptance and recognizing that worth isn't defined by local standards but by the bigger picture. Sometimes, you're the right person or just in the wrong place.

It has been over a year, and I am back in the States. Reluctantly, I left him on another continent. Long distance is now a factor, but I still see that same look when we speak. I can see how he looks at me by the way he talks to me over the phone. I still hear the patience and concern when we talk. He is still supporting my vision. I have found myself depending on his opinion and even waiting for an answer before I move. My goodness, I am trusting him. It's moved past fear, being reluctant, and nervous.

Since leaving there, I have mentored women to become Sisters Arise's leaders. He even had a graduation ceremony, which he attended on my behalf. It has been so easy not to make the tough decisions and place them in his lap. But is that what I was called to do? If it is my vision, I say God gave me to steward, so why am I turning it over to someone else? Building a ministry and a relationship has become a challenge. A challenge that requires tough conversations. 'I ain't gonna lie.' Sometimes, the decisions I make are confusing to me. Do I depend on him because I care about and trust him, or do I depend on him as a steward of the will of God? The line can blur.

We are back to the same two things: trust and love.

I had to search myself for self-love. I love and accept who I am. I love the woman I have become, and if anyone else doesn't, they can kick rocks. I mean, kick rocks. Yes, that is what I have learned. I didn't always feel this way, but life has been a training ground over the last ten years. Circumstances have demanded growth. So yes, I love myself. Then that leaves trust.

Decisions can cause stress.

I remember one day; I was having tough conversations. I was leading with my emotions instead of logic. I stopped in the middle of a logical discussion to have a pity party. I wanted everyone around me to join the party. That didn't happen. However, Mr. Opportunity asked if I wanted him to stop handling the business. I was required to deal with my emotional meltdown. I begrudgingly said no. Then, I complained to Dr. Youngblood that I wasn't being treated fairly. He was having his usual logical self-step forward. Dr. Youngblood will tell you to have your pity party. Just don't invite guests. I hear Doc in my mind, reminding me that stress can kill. I called a friend. She listened, and in the middle of the conversation, I had what I believed was a panic attack. I had never had a panic attack, but it felt exactly like what I heard other people talk about. My breathing was labored, my mind was foggy, and my memory was short. My friend Ava told me to walk away from what I was doing and breathe. Take my mind off what we were talking about and just be. There is no need to speak; sit and be. Be quiet. Be present. Just be. Just be.

What About Him

That emotional shutdown was a wake-up call. It was time to get my head out of the clouds. Stop trying to live in the story of Jenni and Steve and face reality. I am a visionary. I am the leader of the Sisters Arise Movement. I know how to manage a program and the outcome I desire. A few days later, I decided to take my power back. I spent the weekend writing out my execution plan and sharing it with Mr. Opportunity. A real plan with pen and paper. Something tangible that we can both see.

That left me with the decision of what to do about Mr. Opportunity. This decision didn't come quickly. It took a lot of conversation and lots of prayer time. I even shed a few tears.

As I close out this story, I am proud to say I didn't choose Mr. Opportunity. I chose me. I decided to accept love, joy, and satisfaction for myself. I realized that if I allowed myself to be loved, I might find happiness and a healthy relationship.
Don't give up on love. Just start with loving yourself.

The power of self-love and personal choice shapes one's happiness. This reflects a journey of self-discovery, where the focus shifts from external validation (choosing Mr. Opportunity) to internal fulfillment (choosing oneself).

By choosing self-acceptance, love, joy, and satisfaction, I acknowledge that happiness doesn't come solely from another person; it begins within. This realization is transformative because it challenges the idea that relationships alone define happiness. Instead, it emphasizes that true love and healthy relationships are only possible when one first values and loves themselves.

I am excited about the possibilities of love and healthy relationships. If you are like me, you can't wait until book two to see how it goes. For now, the choice is made. Like Jenni and Steve, you may catch us in a remote place enjoying the peace of love. I may reveal his name in book two. For now, enjoy his character— I know I will.

I captured the first day we met in person in words. I hope you enjoy reading as much as I enjoyed writing.

Led By the Heart or Guided by Faith

We all struggle with decision-making. Do we choose from the heart, driven by our emotions, passions, and desires? Or do we make them based on faith, trusting in something greater than ourselves, even when we don't fully understand the path ahead? Consider how many times you've faced choices that tugged at your heart. Often, these feelings pull you in one direction. Typically, the same behavior leads to the same outcome. This isn't just about right or wrong; it's about what guides us. Are we allowing our emotions to take the lead, or are we willing to step out in faith, even when it doesn't make sense?

Please reflect on this: Are your decisions shaped by your feelings or beliefs? It matters, but it does not matter more than your power—it's called wisdom, using what you've already experienced to make that one decision that will change everything.

My lover, My king, My everything.

The day we met was a fantasy come true.

My nerves were on edge; I didn't know what to do.

That day, my heart said, I want to give him a child.

At my age, that sounded wild. You walked through the door; the distance was finally gone.

It was better than anything I could have imagined.

I felt your charm.

When you smiled, I knew I was home.

Your eyes met mine, and I saw the key to all my dreams and goals.

Then you took me into your arms for a strong, warm embrace. I felt protected and free from harm, and now I am safe.

The sound of the drums vibrating my ears.

Louder and louder, almost bringing tears.

The sound of happiness, joy drowned my fears.

Hold on for dear life is all I heard; do not let go; he is the one.

I never wanted this to end; for a moment, time stood still, and I heard the drum calm to a soft melody.

From my lips escaped a gentle sound of relief.

Beat one, beat two the drums sounded so sweet.

From calm to intense, they rolled with ease.

Mending years of pain, trauma, and defeat.

A moment I never experienced and never thought I would see.

It was at that moment that our future had promise because, at that very moment, our hearts became one.

The drumbeats rolled, announcing the entrance of the new king and queen.

Our home is now our castle, and you are the king, and I your queen.

A place where our love will reign.

I am now complete, ready to serve; I hold your hand, I hold your feet.

With love, I give you, my pledge; I am your hands, and you are my head.

As God has ordained since the beginning of time, I will cherish, honor, and support you until the forever bell chimes. I am yours; you are mine.

We are one until the end of time.

My love, my king, your queen, my everything.

Chapter 12: Accepting Love

The importance of embracing love, not just from others but also from ourselves, is the reason to accept love. Often, we struggle with accepting love due to past wounds, self-doubt, or fear of vulnerability—true love, whether romantic, familial, or self-love, requires openness and trust. No one owns love. But by accepting love, they open the door to joy, connection, and healing. Accepting love means embracing our worth and allowing ourselves to experience the beauty and fulfillment that come with it. Many wonderful things are inside love.

Accepting love after a life of trauma and pain can be challenging, but it's possible with the empowering tools of self-awareness and intentional healing. When used with determination, these tools can lead to a profound transformation in your life, instilling a sense of hope and motivation. The power lies within you to overcome your past and embrace a future filled with love and healing.

I am sure you are like me and have often heard that time heals all wounds. I believe that what most people think about healing is suppressing. Especially women, we usually think if we are quiet about the pain and just let it "blow over," it will go away in time. It's like how children hide under the covers when they're scared at night, thinking a monster is in the room. If they stay entirely still or hide under the blanket, maybe the monster won't see them.

We are learning that this isn't true. One of the books I recommend to everyone I work with is *Feeling Buried Alive, Never Die* by Karol H. Truman. In this book, she explains how suppressed feelings, those emotions we push down and try to ignore, never disappear; they linger in your body and cause physical ailments. Suppressed feelings are the emotions we avoid or try to bury, often because they are painful or uncomfortable. These feelings don't go away on their own. They can manifest as physical symptoms or contribute to mental health issues. For example, a person who pushes down feelings of anger may experience increased stress and anxiety, which can lead to physical health issues over time. Similarly, someone who suppresses feelings of sadness might struggle with depression and find it difficult to connect with others emotionally. These suppressed feelings can create barriers to healthy communication and relationships. If you are ready to be intentional, grab that for the next leg of your healing journey after you complete this book.

I hope you have been journaling or thinking things through by now. If you are like me, you will likely reread it and take notes. If not, this is a good time to start.

Then, the journey begins as you build a roadmap to help you along the way. Keep in mind that healing is not a destination but a journey with a plan. Your healing journey is of immense value. It's a path you walk with the support of others who understand

and care. Remember, you are not alone on this journey. Your journey is valuable, and you are supported every step of the way.

As a survivor of domestic violence, I understand firsthand the challenges faced by those dealing with trauma. This personal experience inspired me to create the Jennifer Y. Merriman H.E.L.P. Program©, a comprehensive initiative designed to provide support and resources for individuals in similar situations. I envisioned this program as a beacon of hope and empowerment and a tool for building life skills and prevention strategies.

The program includes evidence-based components that aid healing, such as personalized therapy sessions tailored to address individual emotional needs. We also offer group support meetings that foster a sense of community alongside holistic practices like mindfulness meditation and EFT tapping, which promote mental well-being. Notably, the incorporation of art therapy allows participants to express their feelings creatively, leading to breakthroughs in processing trauma and enhancing overall emotional resilience. The structured nature of the program guides individuals through their healing journey, equipping them with tools and resources to confront trauma and cultivate self-awareness. Additionally, we include education focused on promoting physical well-being and disease prevention to provide a well-rounded solution.

However, after a year of facilitating the program, I realized that I needed to confront my past challenges. No matter how much we try to forget, the past remains a part of us. I took the step to pause my work and hired a transformational coach, dedicating a year to focus on my inner healing and examine my mental and emotional health. That was when my true healing journey began.

I don't feel a parent ever heals from losing a child. I do believe we learn coping skills to push through. For me, I take a lot of prayer and God's guidance. I am mindful of how much praying and how much I have to do. Prayer without the work is just wishing. I knew that if I wanted to love and trust again, I needed to deal with everything inside me—all of it.

Remember This:

Self-Worth & Healing First – You must *recognize your worth* before fully accepting love. *Trauma can leave deep scars that make you feel unworthy of love.* However, *through the inspiring journey of therapy, self-reflection, and personal growth*, you can heal and *believe you deserve love and kindness.* You are worthy, and you deserve to heal and be loved. Your past does not determine your worth; your path to healing and self-acceptance does. You have the power to heal and deserve love once you are healed.

Trauma can overshadow our worth and make us feel less than adequate. But it's important to remember that no matter what you've been through or are feeling, you are worthy of healing and finding love and joy. So, let's step out from the shadows of death.

Let's live with accepting love.

After Jennifer was murdered, I dedicated myself to helping others. I always felt that I could make a difference, so I created the H.E.L.P. Program, which I facilitated in the community. I even began speaking publicly to share my story. I traveled up and down the East Coast, building networks and attending events. Then, one day, I was at a conference on how to get more speaking engagements, a platform I believed would allow me to reach more people with my message of healing and empowerment. The visionary of the event spoke. She said that some of you are moving and shaking and never took time to heal. She said, "You are putting catchy phrases together and bleeding all over the audience." Wow! I thought. What a statement to make to people like me. It's true.

I sat up straight, my ears tuned in more to her tone than her words. That was indeed a moment of self-evaluation. Was this me? Have I covered all my grief and trauma in the disguise of helping many? Was I letting my busy work make me think I was dealing with all my past trauma?

The rest of that weekend, I had to take a good look at what I was doing and who I was affecting with my suppressed pain. I might need to deal with a few things, so I started reading books. I remember the book about feelings buried alive, and I went through that. I started listening to women on stage tell their stories, and I heard the pain in the stories—the unhealed pain.

The Power of Pain

One day, I was sitting on stage in South Carolina, USA. In this particular event, all the speakers were seated on the stage, and one after the other told their stories of childhood abuse, domestic violence, rape, and many other tragic events. On this particular day, I was able to watch the audience. I had just spoken to many of them. They each arrived happy and cheerful. Yet, as each lady told her story of pain, I saw life draining from the audience. It started like a small leak and turned into a faucet. I saw some start to slump in their chairs. Some became fidgety, like they were reliving their trauma. Others, I saw anger, like they wanted to kill the assailants that had caused these speaker's pain. That day, I knew I would never grace that stage again without reaching a certain level of healing. The audience deserves that. They deserve me not bleeding all over them.

I did some research, and that led to the transformational coach. I also worked with a friend who was a therapist. What I discovered is I hadn't dealt with the death of my oldest daughter. I had not dealt with many things. There were many other things I had compounded underneath the death of Jennifer. I carried all of this on stage with me. It made me vulnerable to receiving negative comments. I realized that living in the shadow of others meant I could avoid being seen. This way, no one could hurt me if I remained invisible. It also marked a time of spiritual awakening.

The twenty-third Psalm has always been one of my favorites. I never knew why until I had to walk through the shadow of death. For me, that was the nightmare of the death of my children. It was also the feelings that came after. During this time, I discovered myself. I am in my late 40s and found I am worthy of being loved. In my mind, I was confident of my reason for being.

Remember, Healing is a Journey

Healing is a journey that doesn't always need a destination. It just needs the journey. Becoming aware of my worthiness didn't fix the problem. It gave me a reason to fight for happiness, a level that I aim to Turn into joy.

I made significant changes when I returned to the speaking circuit and hosted events.

1. I established platforms to shape the narrative, particularly regarding how stories are shared. Each of my speakers receives training on healing and protecting the audience. I encourage them to share their experiences from a place of healing rather than focusing solely on their pain.

This approach has made a significant difference for those who hear their stories.

2. At each event I host, I always have a licensed therapist or counselor present who will work with individuals who may need to talk during or after the event, especially when working with youth. I have never spoken with youth with whom I didn't have at least one self-disclose after an event.

3. I added a speaking coach to my programs to help others tell their stories confidently.

4. I am continually seeking ways to advance my journey. As you have read, my personal life has remained in the vulnerabilities of shadows despite excelling in my business. I will eventually come into the light.

I am dealing with the adage, "Practice what you preach." Don't be surprised when you think you have this healing thing on the go; something reveals a new feeling that needs to be released.

When I accepted love, I could not decide about it, so I thought I was okay.

Then, when the situation presented itself, I found myself back at the beginning of all the trauma and pain coming to the surface. I was so glad to have tools and people in my kettle who would pour into me.

Filling Your Kettle

Have you ever heard the saying that you can't pour from an empty cup? Then they usually follow, "What is in the cup is for you, and what comes out is for others." From the moment I first heard these sayings, I could not accept them. In my mind, I don't want to serve you from my cup.

Secondly, I don't want to retrieve the spilled tea from your saucer, table, or floor. Where is the respect in that?

I love a good tea party. Looking at history, you will see that women have done great things over a cup of tea. Now think about it: How do you serve it if you invite someone for tea? Yes, from a kettle. Each person can have their cup and blend it to taste.

The idea that you shouldn't have to serve from your cup but instead from a shared source, like a kettle, is powerful. I want you to shift the focus from self-sacrifice to sustainability. When we heal, love, or give to others, it shouldn't come at the cost of emptying ourselves. Instead, we should have a continuous replenishment source, allowing everyone to receive what they need without draining another.

And when it comes to healing and accepting love, the tea analogy makes even more sense. Like everyone prepares their tea to taste, healing and love are deeply personal. No one should be compelled to accept whatever is offered without consideration of their needs. Instead, the process should be intentional, respectful, and nourishing.

What does that have to do with healing? Accepting love? I'm glad you asked.

The tools you use for your kettle will take you through each phase of your journey. Your kettle will have resources, networks, books, and flair. This will be anything from your best friend you can count on to listen to those resources that have helped shape your life. Your therapist, preacher, librarian, and the list go on. It even includes comfort foods, favorite breathing exercises, and things of physical enjoyment. These things shape who you are. They can also help you become who you want to be.

Journal Prompt

1. Take time to journal about what's in your kettle. List *things and people that have helped you during stressful times. Include things you have always wanted to try but haven't. Make a list of books you want to read and those you have read and would like to read again or share with others.*

2. Make a list of how you feel right now. Do you feel worthy of the healing you are doing? If not, find someone in your kettle to talk to, such as *a coach or therapist. I know you are worthy. I want you to know it, too.*

It is time to step out of the shadows. The light may seem bright at first, but you will adjust. It will feel good once you accept love. People are waiting for you to heal so you can share your experiences, wisdom, leadership, life, and story of triumph.

You deserve all the love and kindness as you embark on this healing journey.

"Anticipating the Pain, Instead of Accepting the Love"
Go, and love, and be loved.

About The Author

Andrea D. Merriman, affectionately known as Lady A," is a Creative Harmony Coach and Master Domestic Violence H.E.L.P.© Coach who will help you clarify your purpose to create self-harmony and take ownership of your life.

Andrea has survived several family tragedies. She works through the pain of her loss with purpose and passion. Clothed in God s strength, she nurtures her family while sharing her philosophy and techniques with women from their youth.

For over three decades, Andrea has worked with people in stressful situations. She has learned the importance of a holistic approach to empowerment, including journaling and having tough conversations. She is a firm advocate for life ownership and believes this will aid in building a balanced culture in the communities.

Andrea designed the Jennifer Y. Merriman H.E.L.P.© Program to combat the increasing risk of dating and domestic violence. The

H.E.L.P. Program offers Hope, Empowerment, Life Skills, and Prevention methods to women of all ages. H.E.L.P. will inspire you to move with forward mobility from a traumatic past into a brighter and purposeful future.

Andrea is CEO and founder of FLR Global Institute, LLC, an organization that trains servant leaders to build trauma-informed businesses while maintaining their faith and core beliefs.

Andrea also founded Feminine Life Rebuilders (501(C)3) because we need to face the very thing meant to harm us. FLR provides a safe place to learn the skills of resilience, overcoming obstacles, nurturing the positive left in us, and even working toward building a legacy. If not, something will continue to hold us back in a place of being overwhelmed and bond us to the memories of our past.

Andrea believes turning Harm to Harmony is a journey of hope, empowerment, self-care, resiliency, and healing from past trauma. You don t have to take this journey alone.

About The Author

Dr. Raymond Youngblood, Jr., who better to speak on overcoming challenges, developing yourself and those around you that the world's leading small-scale gold miner?

Dr. Youngblood endures the harshest conditions, peculiar situations, and navigates hostile environments in jungles and deserts to extract valuable minerals and metals, including gold and diamonds.

He is the creator of YGB Hybrid Currency, the first currency that combines physical and digital assets, and he continues to reshape the international landscape, defying expectations.

In 2016, the State of Louisiana recognized him through HR-Res-87; Dr. Youngblood is the world's only Black American International Gold Miner. As a visionary, he is dedicated to building family empires, strengthening familial bonds, and creating lasting legacies. Rising from poverty, he transformed his family into a powerhouse, proving that wealth and power are not merely earned but can be strategically built.

Anticipating the Pain
Instead of Accepting the Love

It is a powerful message to explore your depths of hope, life, and resilience. It guides you from pain to healing and reveals that you truly love yourself.

Andrea, known as Lady "A," is a Creative Harmony Coach and a Master Domestic Violence H.E.L.P.© Coach. She teams up with Dr. Youngblood, the world's most elite small-scale gold and diamond miner. Together, they present a powerful message about resilience, transformation, and the life-giving strength within the soul. Their work, "Anticipating the Pain Instead of Accepting Love," is a testament to the beauty that unfolds when we embrace what we truly deserve. It empowers us to recognize our worth, instilling a sense of empowerment and confidence.

Like the rare pink diamond, Lady A radiated untapped strength—resilient, precious, and molded by the struggles that sought to shatter her. In a world where passion can be both a gift and a curse, she confronted the abuse she faced and realized she needed to dig deeper, much like searching for diamonds, to find healing. Her story is a testament to the transformative power of resilience, offering hope and optimism to those who face similar struggles.

Lady A and Dr. Youngblood present a powerful truth: a diamond, one of the strongest materials on Earth, requires immense pressure, time, and careful cutting to reveal its beauty. Similarly, pearls, much like the people in her life, are created when an oyster endures irritation, layer by layer, transforming pain into beauty and showcasing resilience in its purest form. Their combined experiences, such as Lady A's confrontation with abuse and Dr. Youngblood's psychological endurance, can serve as inspiration for anyone facing challenges. The stories illustrate how these elements embrace love rather than pain and how we can all transform our experiences into something beautiful.

Anticipating the Pain—Instead of Accepting the Love

www.ingramcontent.com/pod-product-compliance
Lightning Source LLC
LaVergne TN
LVHW051404080426
835508LV00022B/2961

9 781952 039232